HEARTBREAK UNFILTERED

Praise for Milan Vohra

'Guru of love and laughter.'

—*The Telegraph*

'Milan Vohra owns this genre. She deftly weaves in her masterstrokes.'

—*The Times of India*

'She weaves in various themes. Her writing has intensity without overstating emotions. Peppered with quintessential Milan Vohra wit.'

—*The Hindu*

'Vohra is in top form. Warm, witty, and wistful. Romance is in expert hands.'

—*Outlook*

'Powerful writing. You realise that love, or an approximation of it, comes in several shades of gray.'

—*The Hindu BusinessLine*

'Decoding romance! Her characters reflect real people who you will identify with. You will find pages straight out of your life too. Great for a travel read, or your bedtime read.'

– *The New Indian Express*

'Not many Indian authors have the knack for writing romance and humour as Milan Vohra does.'

—*The Telegraph*

'Milan Vohra may be known as the first Indian to pen a Mills & Boon book, but she has come a long way since then. Woman-centric plots and set in an urban space...right up Vohra's alley.'

—*Hindustan Times*

'Vohra is back with what she writes best – romance with frisson.'

—*Outlook*

'Milan's writing is simultaneously funny and nostalgic.'

—*The New Indian Express*

'Modern romance novels like Milan Vohra's are the innovation we need. They are relatable, tell stories, weave in important conversations (like about consent) and are anything but boring.'

—*iDiva.com*

'Milan Vohra's characters reflect real people whom you can easily identify with and their lives, desires and aspirations. Just delicious humour! A great read.'

—*The Hindu*

'Refreshing to see authors such as Vohra bringing much more diversity to our literature, reaching out to the younger generation with realistic modern romance and humour.'

—*Dawn.com, South Asia*

'Milan writes simply and for India's first Mills & Boon author, her prose is surprisingly devoid of maudlin mush and syrupy sentimentality, though given the theme, it could so easily have gone down that road. Splendidly sketched out characters...high on humour...'

—*The Times of India*

'Romance is probably the hardest genre to write. Realistic characters, reasonable backdrops, rational plotline...it is rare to find a love story which ticks all the boxes or even half of them but Milan Vohra's book manages to tick many of them. The book defies many, if not all of my presumptions.'

—*Dawn.com, South Asia*

'You're in for a barrel of laughs…with Milan Vohra's quirky bunch of characters.'

—*Savvy*

'A must-read for the romantic-hearted.'

—*Verve*

'Best known as India's first Mills & Boon author...Milan Vohra's writing is wacky, witty, and brisk.'

—*The New Indian Express*

'Full of witticisms, contemporary references, humour, urban situations…her books make for a great read.'

—*Bangalore Mirror*

'A mélange of romance, passion and complications characterises her writing but there is also a distinct desi touch to it. An absolute laugh riot…where romance certainly doesn't take a backseat.'

—*The Hindu MetroPlus*

'Vohra's books have an overarching theme of romance, which reflects today's woman who has much more agency.'

—*Medianews4u.com*

HEARTBREAK UNFILTERED

Things nobody told you about love, loss and letting go

MILAN VOHRA

The best revenge is living well. Take back your power!

♡ Milan

RUPA

Published by
Rupa Publications India Pvt. Ltd 2025
161-B/4, Gulmohar House,
Yusuf Sarai Community Centre,
New Delhi 110049

Sales centres
Bengaluru Chennai
Hyderabad Kolkata Mumbai

The stories in the book are based on true stories but care has been taken to anonymize the identities of the characters. The publisher and the author are in no way liable or responsible for any similarity that the characters or events in the book may bear with any person or for any loss or incidental or consequential damages caused to any person or entity, or alleged to have been caused, directly or indirectly, by the contents of the book. The views and opinions expressed in this book are the author's own and the publishers are not in any way liable for the same.

Readers are advised not to take any action or inaction based solely on the contents of this book and to take professional help or advice in relation to their respective circumstances. The publisher and author have used their best endeavours to ensure that URLs for external websites referred to in this book are correct and active at the time of going to press. However, they bear no responsibility for the websites and cannot guarantee that a site(s) will remain live or that the content is or will remain appropriate.

P-ISBN: 978-93-7003-264-4
E-ISBN: 978-93-7003-443-3

First impression 2025

10 9 8 7 6 5 4 3 2 1

Printed in India

For my son Krishna Vohra
You have taught me more about courage than
you will ever know.

For my father K.C. Kartar Dalwani
For the warmth and safety of your unconditional love.
I miss you and always will.

∞

The heart's journey is not linear
It is a fluid loop
Through the continuum of love, loss and letting go
Gradually, almost unnoticed by us, we return to wholeness
Trust that it will happen. Try trusting yourself again

Contents

On a personal note 1

1. 'This too shall pass' and other such bullshit 8
   UNCOMFORTABLY NUMB: RAKHI'S STORY 18
   CARDS WE'RE DEALT: GANGA'S STORY 24
2. How low can you go? And how long can this go on? 30
   OUT, DAMNED TOUCH, OUT: SAACHI'S STORY 41
3. It's negative appraisal time: Of your ex and what you had 52
   SLOW BURN: MANOJ'S STORY 64
   JUST VIBING: SHUBRA'S STORY 71
4. This is a lot more about you, than about them 79
   FLIGHTS OF FANCY: TARIKA'S STORY 92
   CONTROLLED CHAOS: YASH'S STORY 100
5. This one's not on you: The narcissistic personality – Know and NO 107
   CHEMICAL LOCHA: JUHI'S STORY 116
6. Love languages, apology languages: What they add up to 123
   MENTOR TORMENTOR: MANPREET'S STORY 130
   SAPOTA SADNESS: ESHA'S STORY 136
7. Which heartbreak pain trumps which? Is there a hierarchy in pain? 146
   FRIENDS AND LOVERS: MIHIKA'S STORY 153
   MIRRORS CAN LIE: RAMINDER'S STORY 159

8. It is what it is. It is over 166
BETWEEN A ROCK AND A HARD PLACE: NILIMA'S STORY 173
9. Why does love change? Why did I not see it coming? 179
NO COINCIDENCES: ANDY'S STORY 187
OUT OF WORDS: JONATHAN'S STORY 195
10. It's called a detox because it was toxic for you 202
POWER GAMES: VANI'S STORY 211
11. The 3-3-3 plan to get you through no-contact 218
HUGS FOR FREE: ARUN'S STORY 230
THE BIGGER PICTURE: VIJAY'S STORY 236
12. What you do with your suffering is your act of resistance 242
MOTH TO A FLAME: SOFIA'S STORY 254
FEBRUARY 13TH, 14TH OR 15TH?: TRIXIE'S STORY 260
13. Closure: The consuming need to meet one last time 270
The Heartbreak Unfiltered Album 287
Thanks Unfiltered 289
Resources 292

On a personal note

∞

So much in life sets us up for the highs of love.

The movies, books, good relationships around us – all fire up our imagination and become our goals. When love appears, we fall headlong into it. And it can be so heady – that instant thrill, that hanging-on-edge feeling of love. Because it feels so right. So, so good. The way your heart hammers when your phone pings and you just know it is him or her. Of course you do. Because you set a special message tone on your phone just for this person in your life. How magical it feels when the phone goes tinnnggg with that beautiful sound! Obliterating every thought in your head till you've seen their latest text. Anything they say, any forward they send, just a link to a song, anything – even an emoticon in response to your last message tells you so much more than just the content of that text. It tells you this special person is thinking of you. Their wit, witty or not, makes you smile. God help that friend who dares tell you that your precious darling isn't as sparkling as you claim. Your heart, that very same heart that you thought was incapable of looking past the annoying qualities of every person you met, has decided to embrace this one person in a completely unquestioning way. You marvel at the beauty of every line of their body, the shape of their fingers, the utter edibility of their ears, the timbre of their voice, the thrill of remembering the last time you met, the heightened awareness of sitting next to each other at a movie, at a café, thighs pressed together along the length of your legs, so alive, so grateful for this moment, with this person.

Nothing could feel righter.

Until it goes wrong.

Because nothing, absolutely nothing, prepares us for the low when love ends inexplicably.

Why is it that you never saw it coming? How could you not have had any inkling at all? How? When did it change? What did you do wrong? What could you have done to stop it? There was nothing, not the slightest hint that this would be the last time for both of you.

It is over. Your heart knows it. Yet it refuses to believe it. The feel of those arms wrapped around you as you lay together that time is still so real. Had they already decided this was going to be the last time? Why didn't you have a say in it? You can still feel the warmth, the smell of them, their breath, the way they pulled you in closer, shifting their body with yours in sleep.

Months later you are still going over it, over and over again. Kicking yourself for the innocence with which you believed this was true, that it was not something casual, that this time it was going to last. That there was an 'us'.

So how could it suddenly be over like that? Poof! Just like that. How could they be gone from your life? The pain of it is physical and excruciating. Instead of time helping you heal, you still spend so much time going over everything, again and again – the feeling of being rejected, of 'not being good enough' for them to choose to stay. You oscillate between feeling an electric pain within you that can sting you to tears anytime and a numb lifelessness as you go about your day.

If any of this rings true, then it is not a coincidence that you are here at this point in time, reading this book.

You know me as a romance writer. I know life isn't all rainbows and sunshine. That's why I like to write stories that are believable, about people who have emotional baggage, who eventually do overcome their issues, despite everything. The 'despite everything' is the important difference. Despite losing your ability to trust another person or trust your own judgement again, despite the despair, despite feeling like life singled you out to be let down, or that it's too late for you now, despite, despite, despite. Heartbreak is part of what comes when you open your heart to love. So if heartbreak is the other side of love, we should never forget that *love hasn't gone away. It is waiting for you – on the other side. Waiting for you to turn the heartbreak around.*

This book will help you understand why love can go wrong, why it hurts so bad, and what we can do differently, so love finds us. (Notice, I didn't say we find love. No. *Love finds us* when we understand what we need to do differently.)

Reading this book will help you make sense of what

happened, identify what you could maybe have changed if you understood yourself better and what you couldn't have changed. It is based on long conversations that I've had with experts, and research to understand the psychology of heartbreak – like why our brain is wired to fall in love, why we keep repeating patterns, and how you can use this horrible heartbreak to create something. Something that'll last long after your tears have dried and that ex has exited your heart. It'll happen.

Writing this book made me realise:

One, pretty much nobody is spared from heartbreak. Regardless of age, education, where we live, first world, third world, secret relationship, open romance, short term or one that lasted a long time, virtual, long distance, an almost relationship, situationship, whatever.
Two, each person's experiences and circumstances are unique. As is their path, process, and pace of healing.
Third, and most important. While each of us believes that this one experience has left us totally shattered – healing *does* happen. Gradually. And with help. All the advice of your friends can only do so much. You have to want to be free of this heavy-heart feeling that hasn't left you since it ended. It can only happen when you decide 'Enough. I'm sick of being miserable. I want to see that old, happy me.' You know it's there, inside you.

This book won't give you gyaan. It'll give you clarity and a plan – to shake you out of your apathy, talk you out of make-up sex, pity sex, revenge sex, rebound love, rethink that urge to meet the ex, make you laugh through your tears and get perspective.

If you can read just a few pages of this book every day, you will realise that you're not alone in this. Honestly, there is hope. We'll get through this together. How? Fair question.

I'm going to ask you to do one small thing, if you want to get over the ex and get on with your life.

Jot down your heartbreak story anywhere, on your phone if you prefer, as if you are telling it to a close, trustworthy friend. Begin today. Begin anywhere you like. *Don't overthink it.* It'll be useful as you go through this book. If you feel you can't do it right now, that's ok too. No stress.

I want you to look at this book in your hands as a sign of hope. That one day, not far from now, you will think of that person who broke your heart. And to your amazement, you will realise it is not painful any more.

Wow. You are finally free of that dull ache you carried around inside you.

Believe me, it does happen. It will happen for you too.

Love will find a way back to you.

With a big hug from me,
Milan

Rewind, Pause, Play

EXIT THE HEARTBREAK *EXperience*

Think of it as a 'Dear diary'. Write down whatever comes to your mind about your relationship. From start to finish. (It could even be in bullet points. It doesn't have to be long.)

Step 1: Set the stage: Find a quiet, private time and place. Minimize distractions. Don't postpone it though. Get started.

Step 2: Choose your medium: Grab any notebook, your phone – whatever feels comfortable. Don't overthink it. Do it as if you're telling it all to a good friend. If you like, think of me as that friend (I'd be honoured).

Step 3: Rewind to the beginning: No matter how those details make you feel, don't hold back. Don't worry about the sequence or language or length (this is not an essay you're submitting). It's a diary for your reference. N*o one is going to read this except you.* (Keep it somewhere safe, though.)

I've listed a few thoughts below to nudge you along.

Recall the initial spark: How you met, your first impressions, what attracted you to them. Things like their laugh, their opinions, their style. Your gut feeling about them. What you told others about them. *The happy phase:* Capture the excitement. Your hopes. Anything that felt especially good or odd at any time. Your precious moments like the first time you held

hands, the first kiss, the first 'I love you'.
Step 4: Pause at the middle: Jot down *significant milestones.* Like major decisions, trips, meeting families, moving in together. The dynamics – your interactions then. The strengths and recurring stress points. Any early incidents you downplayed? Detail them. Also *note the good moments.* How did they support you/ how did you support them in tough times? Did *you* specifically change?
Step 5. Play out the ending: Describe the break-up. Who initiated it? Detail t*he break-up conversation* as objectively as possible. What did you do immediately after? How did you cope in the first few days/weeks? *Post-break-up contact:* If there was any, describe it – calls, texts, chance encounters.

This is your diary, where you document things that you think are important. Everything you put in here will be useful to you. No one is looking at it. You're doing this for you.

1

'This too shall pass' and other such bullshit

There will always be people who think they are being helpful by sitting around you with a serious face, doling out platitudes like 'time heals everything' or 'this too shall pass'. Or worse, the ones who bombard you with trite messages about self-love if they know about your break-up. Of course things like that can get under your skin, but remind yourself: I will not let it get to me. Let me assume people actually mean well. Because most people genuinely have no idea how painful heartbreak can be – physically, mentally and emotionally. They do not understand that this 'feeling sick to your core' state you're in is not just psychosomatic (part of it is, yes, but not entirely). It is not about you not trying hard enough to 'snap out of it'.

The pain of heartbreak is real. That constricted feeling in your chest, the palpitations that you may face out of nowhere, the listlessness, the apathy, the excessive sleeping or absence of sleep, the bloated feeling in your stomach or an over-sensitive tummy – these symptoms are all too real and debilitating. It is not unusual for a person going through heartbreak to experience some of them. If you've noticed any of these changes in yourself (after a life event like the end of a relationship, even if it was short-lived), please know this is not entirely about you wallowing in sorrow or over-imagining the pain your body is going through.

Heartbreak causes a physical, mental and emotional response; a lot like love did.

Heartbreak can affect your body, mind and behaviour just as seriously as an actual physical injury or a life-changing traumatic experience. This was actually researched and proven by Helen Fisher and Lucy Brown. To understand why heartbreak hurts so much, we have to look at love. Why on earth do we fall in love? Sometimes again and again.

First of all, let me tell you – falling in love is not something to beat yourself up about. (Falling in love and repeating old patterns or mistakes is a different story, which we'll come to later.) But I repeat, just the act of wanting love and falling headlong into it is part of our brain's age-old need for survival. *Survival, you ask?*

According to Fisher and Brown, romantic love is hardwired in the human brain's neural circuitry. Love is not just some fuzzy feeling. It's a biological driver, built within our brain. It is a need, as critical to our survival as hunger and thirst, and rooted in evolution. It's like your brain's on a *serious* mission. Think of it like a survival instinct, pushing you to connect with someone. Why? Because, way back when we were cavemen and cave women, connecting meant babies, and babies meant the human race kept going.

That's not all. Love is linked in the brain with a

reward system. It's like your brain's got these 'love zones' – little hotspots that light up when you're head over heels in love. There's a part of the brain, the VTA – the 'pleasure centre', which is like a dopamine factory. It starts pumping out the good stuff when you're around the one you have your heart set on. That's what makes you feel all giddy and excited. Then, there's the caudate nucleus, your brain's 'obsession centre'. It's where all those thoughts about your darling get stuck on repeat. Ever get that 'can't-stop-thinking-about-them' feeling? That's the doing of the brain's caudate nucleus. (I curse mine for being over-efficient!)

And, of course, there are the hormones – the chemical messengers behind the scenes. First, there's 'lust', driven by the sexy hormones. Then comes 'attraction', all about that dopamine-fuelled focus. Finally, there's 'attachment', the warm, fuzzy feeling that comes from oxytocin and vasopressin. That's what keeps you bonded long-term with someone.

So please, stop beating yourself up over falling in love. It was actually your brain doing its primeval thing, pushing you to connect, feel good, and stay together. And here's the thing, the pushback to being denied what felt good, is also centred in responses in the brain. Like a baby, snapped out of a beautiful, cosy sleep, when its pacifier is pulled out abruptly from its mouth. Of course the baby will be agitated and bring the roof down. It needs to feel safe and comfortable and the pacifier which was doing the job has suddenly been taken away. Your brain, deprived of love, is like that furious, red-in-the-face baby who needs its pacifier and needs it now, to feel comforted. Again, this reaction is inbuilt into the brain.

Love is an addiction. When the brain doesn't get its fix – the result is withdrawal symptoms.

In my worst times of crisis, I look to logic to cope. Logic may not help anything immediately, but it does its job slowly. It gives us something to hold on to in that state of feeling helpless – to make sense of things that aren't in our control. For example, why is your heartbreak messing this way with your body, your sleep, your gut, your emotions, just about every aspect of you? Here's the scientific explanation. Romantic-love-activated brain regions are associated with reward and addiction. So, *when love is lost, the brain experiences a kind of acute withdrawal.* It may sound extreme but this is based on facts. Both these situations, being in love and being an addict, cause the release of dopamine. The reward centre in the brain is stimulated and for the person in love, it directly gives a sense of pleasure. But when love is taken away, the brain still needs the dopamine jolt – which isn't coming. We come crashing down. The result is intense pain, withdrawal and craving.

It's a double whammy because soon even the hormones are affected. *Heartbreak depletes endorphins which are natural pain killers.* This is what actually causes that real pain a person may go through with heartbreak. And then heartbreak increases cortisol, a hormone secreted by all the adrenal glands. This can actually lead to changes in weight or a weakened immune system. So you may find that when you are going through a heartbreak, you have more frequent colds or infections. You see? You weren't imagining it. The intense craving, obsessive thoughts, emotional distress of heartbreak all have a neurological basis.

All important events, good and bad, are imprinted in the brain. Just because you had a break-up, the brain's reward systems didn't stop working. They are very much active, still seeking the rewards of the relationship. In fact, the brain perceives the loss of the relationship as a threat and loss of identity. It becomes a horrible conflict between what the brain desires (a reunion) and the reality (of separation). In simple words, *that pain you're experiencing is as if your brain is wailing internally; much like the baby bawling about the missing pacifier that felt so good to it.*

In some very rare cases, heartbreak can literally break your heart.

When I was writing my first book, my editor in the UK and I had been going back and forth on the backstories of the characters. I had outlined some possible causes for the hero's mother dying early in life, in fact soon after his father's death. The editor suggested 'Maybe she died of heartbreak?' I was stunned. Was that even a real thing? Today I know it is. An extreme bodily response to heartbreak can actually lead to heartbreak syndrome or cardiomyopathy (also known as takotsubo). When the mind and emotional heart are hurt, the body sees this as a form of threat, which triggers a fight-or-flight response to release a surge of stress hormones, including adrenaline. So, this is not just someone making drama out of nothing. Far from it. There is actual research which shows that excessive adrenaline rush as a result of heartbreak can actually lead to chest pain, shortness of breath, damaged heart muscles and *in very rare cases,* even death.

For now, forget that happy-never-after. Right now, focus on making a beginning.

We all grew up reading that fantastical story about kissing a few hundred frogs before finding the prince (or princess), didn't we? Well, could you please park the ending that wasn't exactly happy – for now? Just for now. I'm talking about your finding *a mental health therapist who can be there for you. Like no love or lover can.* Look at it as the today version of kissing a few frogs/ therapists, (definitely do not take this advice of kissing therapists literally) as the way to give your story a chance to begin again. If you don't have a therapist, start asking trusted friends for references. Don't give up if the first or second or third one doesn't do it for you. I've been there, done that. Try out a few to find one who works best for you, but persist! Also, don't take any pain you are experiencing lightly. See a doctor and check out what could be causing your symptoms.

Can you stop being your own biggest bully?

Let me spell it out, because it's important that someone does. When you're picking up the pieces, the sneaky, hard part isn't just dealing with the ache in your chest. It is learning to be *good to yourself* along the way. Most of us have spent years being our own inner tyrants.

We're Olympic-level self-critics, beating ourselves up for everything – our poor decisions and indecision. We hold ourselves to these crazy-high standards while giving everyone else a free pass. You *cannot* heal in a place where you're constantly tearing yourself down.

You might think you're being strong; that you'll power through. You figure that beating yourself up will somehow make you snap out of it. Nope. All it does is keep you stuck in the same loop you're desperate to break free from. Your constant, negative self-talk is only keeping you stuck, like the wheels of a vehicle trapped in the mud, spinning in the same place.

Enough already. I need you to *take a tough stand – to be gentle with yourself.* It may feel weird at first, maybe even a little weak, because it's the opposite of everything you've been taught. But real strength isn't about how much pain you can take; it's about not letting pain get the better of you. And if being gentle with yourself, letting yourself breathe, letting yourself off the hook sometimes is the strategy for it, stop fighting it.

Are you ready to treat *you* the way you always wished *that* person had?

That's the real work here. Stop beating yourself up for what is in the past, for things you wish you could undo, for not being perfect (newsflash: nobody is!) Why should turning that same kindness inward feel so difficult? You gave your gentleness to others so easily. And especially to *that* person. Why do you feel like you don't deserve it? That you need to continue to suffer? You don't. Seriously. *Gentleness is not a postponable goal*; it's a must-have, now!

You wish you hadn't been kept in the dark by that person, right? Think back on all the times you wish they had been straight with you. How about making this commitment to yourself right now?

Promise yourself: I am not going to be an asshole to myself. I will keep the promises I make to myself. I will be better to myself than they were, because I bloody well deserve it.

So, how do you actually get there? To that place where things finally start to shift.

You start by making a personal manifesto for yourself. I've explained how to do it on the next page. It'll take you 5 minutes, max.

The 'new me' manifesto

EXIT THE HEARTBREAK *EXpress*

Today, we're going to write your personal manifesto. This is a powerful tool that will help you define the core essence of who you are. More critically, at this time, it will help you shift your focus from what you lost, to what you really value and seek. You don't want to stay stuck being the person you were in that relationship. To shape an identity that feels more authentic to who you are today, you have to set goals as your guideline. Start by defining these two things:

1. What you value 2. What you seek

Step 1: W*hat you value:* Think beyond superficial traits. Identify your non-negotiable core values. Focus on your boundaries and aspirations that are important to how you view yourself. Draft out clear, concise statements (on your phone or wherever convenient) using opening phrases like 'I am', 'I will', 'I believe'. Here are some examples to help you think through and write what you value: Like, 'I believe in mutual respect, where both our voices are heard and valued'. Or, 'I am a person who stands by my friends but only for those who have my back too'. Or, 'I will keep my standards high about who I allow into my life'.

Step 2: *What you seek:* Think carefully. What does your ideal partnership feel like? Setting expectations is key. It could be 'I deserve a partner who consistently shows up, emotionally and physically'. (Add financially to that, if it is critical to you.) Ask yourself what your deal breakers are. A sentence like 'I will communicate openly and honestly, even when it's uncomfortable', reflects your commitment to active participation. Be sure to write a line about your expectations on boundaries clearly. For example, 'I will not tolerate disrespect or emotional game-playing'. Remember, this is not meant to be an essay, it is not for anyone else to see. But these few, well-thought-out, powerful sentences that *you choose to make your manifesto* will become your principles; something like a compass to guide you and course-correct, if need be, to build the meaningful, supportive relationship you deserve.

Finally, narrow it down to the two most important sentences from Step 1 and Step 2.

Write in bold, capital letters, on top of a clean white sheet of paper:

The new me: <add your name>

<The defining sentences that you have chosen as your personal manifesto.>

Stick this up in a place where you will see it many times every day.

Uncomfortably numb: Rakhi's story

All my relationships have shaped me in some way.

The first guy I got involved with was Dhruba, when I was in class 10. He was my age. We were both around fifteen or sixteen when we got involved. But soon I realised he had incestuous tendencies. I had no clue how to deal with it, though he kept sharing things like his creepy feelings for his mother. I thought it was a psychological condition which he could resolve with professional help. Then he started developing an attraction for my mom. He would also say some seriously scary stuff like, 'You only belong to me, Rakhi. Only I should be looking at you.' I realised what an insane road lay ahead of me getting involved with somebody like that. Luckily the wake-up call came in time. And I also moved cities to study music at Shantiniketan.

With the next guy, Nirvik, initially it was really beautiful. This was around the time when I was studying at Shantiniketan. Then I shifted to Kolkata, to pursue music. I used to sing professionally. I met Nirvik through Facebook. He was a nice guy. Quite soon I was in love with him. I went to see him for the first time in Kolkata, then he used to visit me in Shantiniketan. This was the first time that we were alone together. My family wasn't around. Up until then, I was a virgin. I was scared also. I started realising that I wasn't familiar with him. It was strange because our relationship started at around nineteen or twenty but close to two years had passed chatting on Facebook and him visiting near Shantiniketan. He had already started talking about marriage. In person, I felt I just wasn't familiar with him, that familiarity came only when we were texting a lot. And distance mei it was good, with video calls, etcetera, but in person it just felt weird. I started feeling pressured because the whole thing was building into an expectation that I would marry him.

Around this time, I met Kaushik who was twelve years older than me and in the music industry. He would keep telling me that he had fallen in love with my voice, that he couldn't imagine what it would be like to live with a nightingale like me in the house. All that flattery felt really good and I fell hook, line and sinker for it. I was conflicted also because the guy I was expected to marry was in the same city. Yet now I had gotten involved with this much older guy and also ended up having sex with him. For me, the sex was also great with Kaushik, basically because I was so much in love with him. Up until the time that we had sex together, I felt I had met somebody who really got me, my soul, because music was my soul. It seemed natural, almost inevitable that the body would follow.

Then he ghosted me. I had no idea why. It was the first time in my life that I was living alone and this business of him ghosting me just made me fall apart. I would go to the places I knew he would be in, in the hope of seeing him or to be able to pretend that I had just bumped into him, to be able to talk to him. I would go crazy. I was in a new university. I was in a new band and there were new dynamics in the girl band. I understand now that it had become more than a psychological issue for me, but believe me, the abrupt way that Kaushik vanished from my life actually had a deep physiological effect on me. I was completely not in control of myself, my music, my commitments, or any of the reasons that had brought me to study at this place. I would stand on the road, feel an extreme burst of anger, and would lose my direction to go home. I would feel like I'm was always inside a mosquito net. I was always struggling. It conflicted between what was going on inside me which I hadn't shared with anybody in my family and keeping up a pretence on the outside with Nirvik and my parents; like nothing had happened. I could not eat. I had become so indecisive. Even if somebody was with me and insisted on ordering some food, I would look at that food when it arrived and couldn't decide whether to eat it or throw it. I had become very anxious and depressed.

Thank God that at some stage my mother got through to me. I told her I needed help, so I got a psychiatrist. The doctor was very supportive. She made me call Kaushik from her clinic. I was shaking and felt he was also nervous as fuck. I was confused about why he was like that. It was a mundane conversation but I broke one barrier. I went to the mirror in the bathroom and I remember that I smiled to myself. For the first time in very long, I felt OK.

I used to love the rain but during that time I

remember I couldn't even feel the rain. I felt like whatever was happening with Kaushik, I would have to just let it play out. But I didn't want things to change with Nirvik.

So I started medication, I started getting a little better. I was paranoid about feeling sleepy; I didn't want anything to make me feel drowsy and even less in control. I would go on to stage with pills to tackle the tremors and the panic attacks.

Then after six or seven months, Kaushik starts replying to my status updates. Before this, I had a dream that he was getting married to the girl he was seeing before me. All of this was just like one psychedelic haze. One highlight in all of this was that Kaushik asked me to meet him at a cafe. I had had a few tequilas and next thing I knew, I said yes to him. I went to the café. I was feeling nervous obviously, when his bike arrived. Just before leaving for the cafe, I sent him a closure text. I said, 'I don't know what went wrong. No matter what happens, I will always hold a candle for you.'

Then I saw him and it was such a flood of emotions. All that deep deprivation and pining to see him and finally he was in front of me. But in my stomach, I had a sinking feeling. I asked him, 'What do you want to tell me? Are you getting married?' He said, 'Yes.'

All I wanted was to understand what had happened. I burst into tears in front of everyone there. A large part of it was anger. He could have told me earlier and saved me all this pain.

He says to me, 'I've always thought you were a

strong woman. You'll deal with it.' Then – look at the cheek. He says, 'I thought we can continue. But it can't be at my house.'

I have always been loved my entire life. Other women who say we've never been loved, well that's not true for me. Kaushik is still in touch with me; we still do video calls. At least it helped me get clarity about what I felt about Nirvik. The month that Kaushik got married, I broke up with Nirvik because I realised there was no sexual spark.

This happened in 2018. Between then and now, things that have helped me get past it: One, knowing what happened. Two, my music, my music, my music.

Kaushik said that when this other girl came back into his life, he was in love with me. But he says Rocky, our common friend, said I won't break up with Nirvik. That we both have a fear of confrontation. No matter how angry I felt about it then, it did still help that Kaushik told me in person that he's getting married. I went to great lengths to stalk him, to see who's liking his posts and to stalk all those people too. It helped that I made sense of it in my own way. Yes, Rocky was right that we both had issues with confrontation. I have never been good at facing facts or being the driver of my life – no matter how much I wanted to be that way.

I went through a stage of wanting to fuck around. It gets worse. It always does, doesn't it? It's always darkest before dawn. Even if it sounds like a cliche, it is true. My music has saved me. Yes, it's awkward as hell when I run into Kaushik, because the music industry is small. I always feel as if a woman comes off looking bad even if the guy has been equally unclear about what he wants out of any relationship. But music heals. Time helps too.

When I walk in the rain now, if tears escape, so be it. I can feel them. I can feel them and the rain.

Cards we're dealt: Ganga's story

I didn't have the terminology for the conflict I felt with my identity when I was young. Only later, I learned the term for someone like me. A trans man. I'm Ganga Chandra, born with a woman's body, with the feelings and orientation of a man. I fell in love once, with Jyoti, a trainee at a big newspaper. The attraction was immediate.

She was also from Uttarakhand, like me. She's a straight woman. But she felt a strong attraction, just as I did. She said, 'I want to live with you. You arrange everything.' I was twenty-eight, not out yet. Ghar pe people had an idea, but when I told my mother, she said, '*Apne dum pe karlo jo bhi karna hai.*' (You'll have to rely on yourself; do whatever you want to.) In one day, I found us an apartment. She was twenty-two. Despite being a reporter, I was shy and didn't share my feelings much.

Living together felt good at first. We couldn't live without each other. I was the more masculine one. She preferred staying home and I assumed that's how it was. I cut off from my family, except for secret support from my mother. The financial pressure was heavy. Jyoti wasn't earning, and I had to support my younger sister too. For years, it was a struggle even to manage the home. I was overwhelmed with the responsibility and to be fair to Jyoti, she was so young.

She would complain, 'I have to guess everything about you.' I spoiled her, gave her whatever she wanted.

I come from a broken family. Papa died young, my mother had struggled a lot. I was determined to make it work between us. I ignored the problems. In the eight years it lasted, so many times we broke up, made up, broke up, made up.

Earlier, if she left, she'd return. She had never been in another relationship. I had dated other women, but never thought of commitment. They were usually intellectuals, never a simple, young girl like Jyoti. My attraction to her was instant.

Until I met her, I had never thought of living together or having kids. I wanted them but my communication was bad. I feel like I couldn't make her feel secure or relate to any of my needs. She was also very possessive. I would say to her so often, 'Instead of being suspicious, why don't you work? I don't care about salary. Start building a life for yourself.'

One time, only in anger, in an outburst I said, 'I don't want to live with you.' She moved out, then came back, then left again. It was so tiring. Finally in 2016, she left for good. The fight that broke us for good was over finances and it kept getting extended.

She kept reaching out, saying 'Let's get back.' By then I had moved back to be with my family. All my friends had been quite categorical in telling me that Jyoti was using me. I started to think more and more about community and in what way I wanted to give back to my community. Initially when we were apart, I started feeling relief. It was not as if we cut off completely. We'd be in touch. I would keep telling her, 'Look, start working please.'

Six months passed. Again, I looked for an apartment, thinking we'll figure it out. If we got back together, I'd have to stop helping my mom with the rent.

Around then, my sister forwarded some detailed chats to me and I saw that Jyoti had been flirting with some married guy. It was a huge shock. For six months, Jyoti had been pushing me to move back. And then I get to know, this has been going on. The man's wife is planning to sue her.

Earlier I used to tell Jyoti, 'If you want to explore the other side, leave me out of it.'

This time, I exploded. I confronted her. She said, 'I'm being framed.' I said. 'At least admit you made a mistake. Then I can help you.'

Finally, I saw the truth. She's a straight woman. The problem wasn't just me. It was that she isn't clear about her identity. I understood that this can't go any further. I can't be in her way. I felt so inadequate. This was something I could never give to her. If she wanted to find a relationship that was straight and heterosexual, come on, how could I ever give her that?

I didn't say anything to anyone. I stopped eating. Only then I realised how much I loved her and how close we had been. I am a liberal person. I said so often to her, 'Only if you love me, we will be together.' I would keep crying in the middle of eating. People would be astonished at home. It had been such a long relationship and one that I had taken for granted. I had never held back from giving her anything she wanted. But this was out of my control.

It completely broke me. I started visiting one ashram after another. I wanted to end my life.

On one hand I would be in touch with her. We would talk like strangers. I would be like a cold person. I started feeling the other side only is better for her. I considered suicide so often. Luckily I didn't go ahead with that, but the thought would often come to me. I started random back-to-back dating, which also screwed up my mind. It never got me what I wanted either – a committed relationship. Girls would either say bye-bye very fast, or they would get obsessive. I would keep getting shocked by these situations.

In 2018 Jyoti got married to a guy from Haldwani, which is my hometown. It totally fucked me up. I was not able to focus on anything. Even the crappy relationships ended. After eight years I moved back home during the pandemic. I would stay in my room all day. Through this long bleak period and not being able to see any happy solution to my life situation; the way I was born and the way I had blown up my one long solid relationship – thank God, I had my mom. She kept saying it's OK if you don't earn. One good thing – my relationship with the family became stronger. I started realising these other relationships were doomed because of my own identity issue, the hopes I had and their mismatch with the women I would meet.

After the sorrow of the final break-up with Jyoti and seeing her get married, I gave up all that journalism shit. I realised that all the importance I attached to being an intellectual, hanging out with intellectuals and the shallow dating that I was doing, judging other people on their lack of awareness, was not making me any calmer or happier. I wanted to pursue my spiritual side. Somewhere, somehow, I got into yoga and did some courses. I didn't realize I was growing through it. In 2019, I developed irritable bowel syndrome (IBS). I couldn't digest simple boiled dal. I started to teach yoga but was always low on energy. I started meditating seriously, four times a day, like my life depended on it.

That's when I started opening my heart and exploring community. Till then I hadn't come out. It was only after the darkest period that I started talking about my sexuality. Now I post a lot on Instagram. I realize that had I been at this stage of realization earlier, I might not have stayed in that relationship so long. But the jhatka which my body gave me, in that most bleak and hopeless period when I felt I had destroyed the one long, loving relationship in my life, was both my downfall and wake-up call. So often I would have to cancel my classes immediately because of my IBS. It made me look at what was actually making me so sick. It was my lack of acceptance of my sexual identity and leading a double life, pretending to be someone I wasn't. It was only when I could accept my sexuality that I could see why my relationships weren't working and why my health had continued to be so bad. My IBS improved by at least 40 per cent. I could pick up the threads again to teach yoga.

Then, most significantly for me, because our family is into spiritual things so much, I got interested in tarot. I'm a tarot reader now and it's very fulfilling. Tarot has given me a way to handle the cards I have been dealt and to help other people with their lives.

I feel like my life is just starting. As if everything else before was research, and I was just getting prepared for the actual main movie of my life. All that earlier stuff was like what those Punjabi stud boys do. Fool around a lot, then marry some good gharelu girl. I realised all the earlier stuff that I used to do was stud baazi. Now I feel like I've come home with astrology and a much better understanding and acceptance of destiny and karma.

You get a very short window to change your destiny. About 60 per cent of what happens to you is your destiny. And you really have to put your life into changing things. 'As above, so below.' Heartbreak opened the way to tarot, teaching me this about life. Only by understanding the macrocosm can we gain insights into the microcosm. They are mirrors of each other. Even stars and planets mirror the structure and function of the human body and mind. Just as the stars move in harmonious patterns, so too do the atoms within our bodies.

This is what I feel now. To grow anything, you have to water it, you have to take care of everything. My sister was a tarot card reader and even though I was exposed to it for so many years of my life I wasn't interested then. Now I realize it was my destiny. If a partner is meant for me somewhere in my future, the cards will tell me.

2

How low can you go? And how long can this go on?

You've probably tried a lot of stuff already to mend the relationship. You may even have been desperate enough to try to fix it in ways you're ashamed to admit, even to your closest friend. We've all been there. The low point you've hit, can and will change once you understand what's going on inside you.

When can you hope to recover from this shit experience?

Nobody tells you what's the acceptable amount of time to cry over a broken relationship before you may hope to start to heal. I read formulas like 'a month for every year you both were together' and I say, no, please, no. What is that even based on? Who is to say that a relationship that was decaying over ten years can be cried over in ten months and then off you may go, with all of it forgotten and behind you. Or that a situationship that lasted two months should be less impactful than a long one? Who is to decide for anyone else whether a long-distance relationship break-up is less damaging than one where the partners lived together or saw each other a lot. No one can tell you 'this has gone on too long, stop crying over it.'

Only you can pull back, really see yourself and say 'enough!' Only you can pull yourself out of this miserable black hole. For that, you need to treat yourself with compassion, much better than *that* person knew how to treat you.

What is making you act like this?

Why does heartbreak have the power to damage us so much? There's no single answer to that. I believe, at the core of it, is our sense of complete helplessness in the situation, to not be able to change what happened. Maybe you saw it coming for some time, the way he/she had started acting differently, being less invested in you. Maybe the texts had gone from being spontaneous and high energy, to becoming sporadic and just not the same. And all your efforts felt increasingly one-sided. Or maybe the end came crashing on you right out of nowhere. Maybe it all looked good, and bang! Next thing you know, you learn they've been banging someone else!

How do you recover from the fact that it was not perfect maybe but you still thought you were a unit, you still had hope. And yet, it is over now. Just like that.

What hurts is that *you* had no choice and no voice in the way that it ended.

The powerlessness it leaves you with is the first point I'd like you to consider. So you went all in. You held nothing back; you gave the person your heart fully. And slowly you gave them all the power you had in the relationship.

Now you may well say, Milan, this *is* how I love, I don't like to hold back or play games when I love someone.

And I would first just ask you to go to your heartbreak diary. Read the incidents, especially the early ones, where you can clearly see the power equation being formed in your relationship. Note the ways you gave away your agency, you gave them your power. I am trying to build a logical foundation for us to work with, for you to get through this heartbreak.

Let's talk about the power that you handed away, on a platter.

I am reminded of a conversation that happened a long time ago, in my first job. In those days people didn't think twice before asking personal questions. My boss (known to be quite the Casanova, and an intelligent man) asked me for the nth time, 'So you already have a boyfriend?' 'Yes,' I answered patiently, with an eye roll. Mr IIT, IIM and the Copy chief of the ad agency then asked me, the young copy cub, 'Who has all the power in the relationship?' 'Huh?' I blinked, never having thought of anything like that. 'You guys fight yet?' he continued. I shrugged. The unspoken answer was, 'Of course, who doesn't?' 'And who tends to do the making-up?' he persisted. 'Me,' I said. 'Mostly or always?' He asked, eyebrows raised. 'Always,' I grimaced. It was the truth. Not a truth I liked but it was what it was. I couldn't bear the idea of holding on to a fight and always caved in first. My boss, the proud 'player' and Mr Know-it-all, shook his head. 'Hah,' he snorted. 'Your boyfriend already holds all the cards, darling,' he declared. I thought that idea was ridiculous. Who talks of a real relationship, that had already lasted a few years, in terms of 'holding the cards'.

Ugh. That felt manipulative. At the time I looked at it as typical of my boss and his distorted view of relationships, or their lack thereof. But later I thought, who filled our heads with these notions of 'love comes first' and 'park your ego when it comes to love'? Over time, I realised, his observation didn't seem so off base.

I am not suggesting that we become dogmatic about every disagreement. But what if, for a change, instead of being the one to always bend and 'adjust', what if – sometimes we honour ourselves and see if he/she also tries to see our point of view? To come around to doing something that matters to us. That's what I mean when I say hold on to your power. Let somebody really earn that choice, if you do decide to do something for them. Let it be a choice you make of your own free will, not something that comes from a fear of losing that person or from a need to please them or defuse a situation.

That power hasn't gone away anywhere. Know why? Because it was always yours.

Yes, you gave your heart and your power away to someone, even if it turned out to be the wrong person. But it was a choice *you* made, whether or not you realised it. You could give that power away, only because *it was yours* to give. By that same token, that power, that agency in what you choose to do, now or later, *has to return to you because it only belongs to you.* The first thing to remember is this. The power was always yours. It is yours to reclaim any time you decide to do so.

You will find that you have the power to do it differently

next time. *The power over who you are, what choices you make, who you love again is yours, it cannot go away.* It is sitting inside you – waiting to be summoned up by you.

The point is, do you want to find the will to use your power or hit rock bottom first? Rock bottom is not a pretty place. Life isn't a game of limbo dance. You know, the one where you dance bending lower and lower under a rod, to the chant of the song, 'How low can you go?' Why should you bend to a point where you are set up to fail? Wouldn't you rather cut loose and start your healing?

Every story in this book is your wake-up call to stop.

In many of the stories in this book, you will read of people talking about pleading with their ex to meet just one more time. Some go to great lengths to stalk not just the ex but to stalk the hell out of the ex's next. They torture themselves on loop, looking at the ex's social media, tracking how the ex has moved on; what a great time they are having. In a few of the stories, some people talk about hitting their lowest point, even going on a sex rampage to get back at the ex; to show them what a good time they could also have without them. Others talk of spiralling by constantly revisiting pictures, text messages, past memories, to the point their life feels worthless. There's *no one watching you 24x7 to say don't do this* to yourself. That wake-up call to stop damaging your soul is something only you can do and must decide on. And the reason for it can't be that your friends are going to be mad at you (though for sure the good ones will and should be).

I urge you. Stop bargaining. Stop agonising. Stop. Just stop.

What your behaviour and actions point to is someone in deep grief.

The heart feels the wreckage of a relationship as profoundly as the death of a loved person, or the trauma of losing a limb or the passing away of a beloved pet. It puts all our emotions in a churn. Different people react to grief in different ways. One person may find they are stuck in one stage of grief for very long. Others may feel like they're on an emotional roller coaster, up and down on different loops between the five stages of grief: Denial, anger, bargaining, depression, and acceptance.

What you are going through are the five stages of grief, in no particular order. Pull up your heartbreak notes. Mark out incidents where you could see it going downhill. And some in the 'but is it really over' stage. Please go through the examples I've described below to explain the ways we grieve. *See if you can connect your important, recent incidents to these stages in the grief cycle.* Identifying the 'grief' stage you're in from the trigger and your reactions will help you to accept. It's an important step in being able to break free.

Denial: The 'It's not *really* over' period

Trigger: Seeing their car parked somewhere you both once went to. *Reaction:* 'Oh, they must be here hoping to bump into me. I knew he/ she would be back.' (Even though you know logically they moved out of your life weeks ago.) You might even mentally prepare to greet them, your heart doing a hopeful little flutter before reality hits. *What it does to you (in denial):* Maybe you start avoiding places you used to frequent together, not because it's painful, but because you subconsciously expect to run into them and undo the past. You might also hold onto their belongings, in the hope that they'll need the stuff soon; that the things will bring them back into your orbit.

Anger: The 'Every reminder is an insult' phase

Trigger: A mutual friend mentioning how happy your ex seems in their latest social media post. *Reaction:* An immediate surge of resentment. 'They have the audacity to be happy after what they did and how they left? I bet they're just trying to make me jealous.' You burn up internally, maybe even start to vent to friends about their flaws. *What it does to you (in anger):* You start unfollowing them and all their connections online. You may have started talking negatively about them to anyone who will listen. Maybe you even found yourself actively looking for ways to catch them out, get to their truth, maybe they're unhappy; nothing would make you happier than to discover they're not doing as well as they're 'pretending' they are.

Bargaining: The 'If only I had done things differently' loop

Trigger: A song comes on the radio that was 'your song'. *Reaction:* A wave of what-ifs washes over you. 'If only I hadn't been so critical of their hobbies. If only I had agreed to couples therapy sooner. 'Maybe if I'd just said "yes" to that weekend trip, things would be different now.' You replay past moments in your head, trying to identify the exact point where things went wrong and imagining alternative outcomes. *What it does to you (in bargaining):* You have constant inner regret. You make vague promises to yourself about how you'll be a better partner next time, internalising the blame for the break-up. You might even have fleeting thoughts of reaching out with a carefully crafted message hinting at change, even though you know, deep in your gut, it's likely to be futile.

Depression: The 'Everything feels pointless without them' slump

Trigger: Seeing a couple holding hands in public. *Reaction:* A heavy wave of sadness and loneliness. 'That used to be us. Now I go home to an empty apartment. What's the point in trying to meet someone new? No one will ever understand me like they did.' You might feel a lack of motivation for things you used to enjoy and struggle with feeling isolated. *What it does to you (in depression):* You find yourself withdrawing from social activities, spending more time alone and experiencing changes in sleep and appetite. You keep revisiting old photos or messages, not out of anger or denial, but a deep sense of longing and loss.

Acceptance: The 'It happened, now what?' gradual shift

Trigger: Running into your ex unexpectedly and their new partner. *Reaction:* A moment of discomfort, perhaps a fleeting sadness, but ultimately a shrug of reality. 'Okay, I guess that's their life now. I have my own.' You might manage a polite interaction without feeling overwhelmed. *What it does to you (in acceptance):* Finally you're focusing on your own healing and growth. Engaging in activities you enjoy, spending time with supportive friends and family, and starting to imagine a future that doesn't include your ex. You might still have occasional melancholy moments, but they don't consume you. You're starting to build a new normal.

I hope these examples help you see how the stages of grief continue to play out long after the relationship has ended. Everyday occurrences can and often do trigger and remind you of what you've lost. Understanding is a crucial first step. Even to reach a place where you can look at yourself in a detached way and tell yourself 'Okay I know this is just me, feeling angry about everything. But I need to get past this anger. Or depression. Or denial. *I need to do it because that person sure as hell isn't losing sleep crying over me.'*

I'm sorry, really, I am, for what you're going through. But the truth is: They made it clear; they were not choosing you.

Can you now at least decide enough is enough? No more crying over someone who did not value you enough.

Show up for yourself. You *choose you.*

A helicopter ride

EXIT THE HEARTBREAK
EXpand

Today you are going to revisit that problematic relationship with a helicopter perspective.

Step 1: Get some coloured pens, crayons, colour pencils, whatever is handy. And some sheets of white paper to draw in. Don't sweat it. Let's begin.

Step 2: Draw a scene from the relationship that ended. Don't worry if you're no great shakes as an artist. Neither am I and I have managed just fine a long time in advertising, drawing with matchstick figures. No one is going to see this except you. Imagine you are sitting in a helicopter looking down at the two of you. Let the chopper go up, up, up, up, a little higher still.

Think of a scene from the beginning of your relationship, when love was new and you were expressing yourselves in your love languages. Maybe he was sweeping you off your feet with special gifts. Or she was looking at you with wonder, praising your talent. Add speech blurbs if you like.

Step 3: Draw another scene/s from when you were upset. When they couldn't give you love or an apology the way you needed it. Keep sitting in that helicopter seat. You are viewing specific scenes with your ex that made you feel unseen, or small (making sly put-downs or a high-handed decision maybe). Colour the parts that make you angry with angry colours. Pick what comes naturally. A poisonous purple or a slimy dirty green colour? Go for it. Add additional elements. Is it raining? Are you alone in a car? Or feeling isolated in a crowded bus or metro, looking at your phone waiting for a reply? Draw it out. *Think of it all as if you can see everything, a little like if you were a superhero, looking down at yourself in that scene.*

Step 4: Spread out the drawings on a bed. Stand up. See them like you're still looking from above, from the helicopter window. You have a safe pilot driving you. *Your only job is to throw a lifeline to pull that past version of miserable you* out of the sad scene down below.

Step 5: Draw a rescue line, drop it from the sky, from the helicopter window, to directly reach you in the drawing, to pull you out of the scene. Add another drawing if you like. Let's keep that stupid jerk standing there alone, while you've almost made it into the chopper. What does that look like? That ex. down there. Want to wave? Hmmm. Feel free to add blurbs with cuss words or kind parting words if you like. Me, I'm not forgiving. I know it's a failing. I'd leave that hollow-promise-maker standing there below, with his lying mouth and his fly open. Maybe there are even some flies waiting to get in? I leave the details to you.

Out, damned touch, out: Saachi's story

I was the first in my family to leave Ranchi for the big, bad city of Mumbai. My mother had forever been on my case to 'get settled, get settled, Saachi.' Only the promise of nightly calls to say I was back home, and Ashwin, our family friend's son's reassurance to look after me, finally let the family allow me to step out on my own.

I took well to my new job at a travel agency. My boss appreciated my ability to handle difficult clients. The office gang often went out to get a drink but the one time I'd gone with them, I felt out of place. I preferred to spend my evenings with a good romance film on my laptop. Two years in Mumbai and I was financially independent, even sending some money home. Prabha, my younger sister, had just completed her MBA and had matches coming in, but in Jharkhand, it is not done for a younger child to marry before the older one. My family began insisting on putting up my biodata on a marriage website.

When I ranted about this, Ashwin said it was no different even for men. 'My friend Prashant's family are also like stuck records on this topic. His father put up his profile on a marriage website without asking him! Prashant doesn't want any distractions like marriage. He has two and five-year plans for everything.'

One day Ashwin called, saying his friend Prashant had complimentary tickets to the latest Julia Roberts film.

Ashwin offered his ticket to me because he hates mushy movies. I hesitated. Watch a movie with someone I had never met? Ashwin offered to drop me there and introduce me to his friend. 'You'll love him,' Ashwin said.

The words turned out to be prophetic. Prashant was pleasant looking and just the right amount of friendly. He listened with interest, hardly looked at his phone and offered to drop me back. I found myself offering him chai and pulling his leg about having plans for everything. I asked if it was true of marriage too? 'It's a plan with a contingency provision,' he said. 'For when the right person comes along,' he added clumsily. Our eyes had met just then and it felt so right. A little like the movies. Wasn't that what I had always hoped for?

Our courtship was rapid. Prashant would pick me up from work, drop me home without fail, giving me a quick kiss as he left. I liked how it made me feel. Ashwin hung out more often at my place, with Prashant around. It made me yearn for privacy. It had been three months from the time we met. There was laughter, warmth, especially when Prashant, Ashwin and I were together. I hated it if I didn't hear from Prashant. The thought that he would soon be moving to Pune on a promotion felt awful.

When Prashant proposed, jokingly, 'Let's get our parents to take our biodatas off the shaadi website?', it had been easy to grin and say yes. The wedding happened in a blur. Both families were overjoyed; kundalis and castes – all matched. When he was leaving for Pune, it dawned on me that he hadn't talked about my moving with him. Nor had he said anything about him trying to look for a job in Mumbai. For two months we did the long-distance thing. Prashant felt Mumbai and Pune weren't far; there was no need to change anything. When I relayed conversations about our parents hinting that we try for a kid, he'd brush it off. 'We need time to enjoy being a couple,' he'd say. I agreed but didn't see him translating that into action. More and more, I made the effort to go to Pune to see him. It was tiring and expensive too. I wanted us to be together and was puzzled he wasn't doing anything about it.

Then there was my first Karva Chauth. I wanted to fast for his health, hoping he'd fast for me too, but he told me not to bother. To avoid a fight, I blamed our mothers. He insisted I could pretend to fast and he'd cover for me.

I decided the distance was magnifying our misunderstandings. I asked my boss for a transfer to Pune. She warned me it was a bad career move, but I was willing to take a pay cut and a lower position in the company, if the city move could help make our marriage work. Initially it was quite nice but somehow, I felt Prashant was holding back. There was an emotional distance that I couldn't close. I had never been with any man before my husband. I didn't know what to make of our physical intimacy. The sex made me feel connected and close to Prashant. Yet he never wanted to linger or cuddle. The expression on his face was never relaxed and he would always rush to shower afterwards.

Sex started becoming rarer. I had no way to gauge if this was normal. It was too personal to ask anyone.

I started thinking something about me displeased my husband. Just his look sometimes, unaware that I'd seen him moving across the room, looked far from loving. I'd tell myself I mustn't imagine things. That this phase was about getting used to each other. Sometimes, I would try to initiate making love, but Prashant would take my hand and place it to my side. Silent rejections. Once, after sex, I had even seen him crinkle his nose as he headed to the shower. That time I insisted on asking what the matter was. 'It's too messy,' he said. I had searched on the Internet for what I could do to please a man in bed but found nothing that talked about how to deal with the distaste, not just disinterest, that I sensed in him. I tried to remind myself of his positive qualities like his dependability. How he'd text to check when I'd finish work, and often pick me up from a convenient spot.

One day when I was waiting near his office, Prashant's colleague and I started talking. I discovered she was also new to Pune like me. Prashant drove up to us and the woman said, 'Didn't even know you're married. Your wife's been telling me so much about you.' Prashant mumbled that I always exaggerate. That was the first time we argued. 'Why were you talking to my colleague?' he asked curtly. I couldn't understand what Prashant hadn't liked. I'd only said good things about him. He drove home in a sulk, dropped me off and zoomed away. *What had I done wrong?* It confused me. I felt ashamed. I concluded that he didn't want to be associated with me.

The distance between us kept growing. I put it down to the pressures that came with both of us having a late marriage, especially to give the families 'good news'.

I had assumed that because our backgrounds were similar, we would want the same things. I tried speaking to Ashwin about it. He was always busy, preoccupied with reworking his CV and applying for jobs. He'd lost his job recently. Finally, when we did connect, he asked me to relax. 'C'mon Saachi. Give the guy space.'

I started working later and later hours. Told myself that Prashant had been single longer than I had, the adjustment was tougher for him. Often, I'd take autos after work, get off some distance before the house, to walk and think and delay reaching home.

It had been months since Prashant and I even had sex. Any small thing led to friction. Like once, I found money missing from a bundle of cash I had withdrawn from my salary, to loan to our part time helper. It was money I could ill afford to spare, considering I was working on a reduced package, but as a woman I understood her situation. She desperately needed help. Imagine my shock when I realised more than half the money wasn't there; where I usually keep it. It became a big flare-up when I asked Prashant if he took it by any chance. He escalated it, calling me petty, hyper, suspicious and always making a 'baat ka batangad' (blowing things out of proportion). He insisted that I must have used up the cash on something else and forgotten. I started feeling like maybe I really was all that he called me.

The last time I had tried to initiate sex, hoping it would bring us closer, he again made me feel responsible for his lack of desire. It became like a load I carried around, a continuous feeling of failure, without knowing why.

One particular evening I was cramping, my period threatening to start earlier than usual, I took the auto right up to the house. It was a few hours earlier than my usual time to get home. As I let myself into the flat, I could hear music coming from the bedroom. That was surprising. Prashant had texted me earlier to say his bosses were in town. I wasn't expecting him to be home. Hand poised on the bedroom door handle, I paused, surprised to hear Prashant's voice singing along with this song. And laughing. Along with his voice, I heard another voice and muffled laughter. I opened the door, expecting to see anything but this.

Prashant and Ashwin – in the middle of having sex. The laughter and song froze on their lips as Ashwin's eyes saw me first and widened. Prashant turned from his lover to see me at the door. The image of their naked bodies glistening with sweat, the expression of utter pleasure and that relaxed smile on Prashant's face, the bliss that I had always dreamed of seeing on his face with me - but had never.

They were fucking. And they were laughing and singing while they did it.

The truth unravelled fast. No cover-up, no excuses. It had apparently been Ashwin's idea to get Prashant and me together – to get Prashant's parents off his back about marriage. Ashwin couldn't bear losing his lover to an unknown woman. And then he saw the perfect solution in me. So much started to fall into place for me, even as everything started to fall away. Prashant's distaste for physical contact with me. The missing money – to help Ashwin out, his true love. I didn't matter to him!

So, Ashwin had engineered it. But Prashant had gone along with everything. Had he even tried to make it work with me? My heart felt like it had been pinched in the centre. The shock of what I had seen, the incomprehension, the sense of failure as a woman that the marriage had created in me.

It just didn't help to know that it was not me. That my husband loved another. Another man. Someone my whole family trusted. Our family friend's son. How could I wipe off the shame? Of being an idiot, of making a fool of myself, of giving myself on a platter to the man I gave my heart to. And for him to use me like that. I was consumed with endless questions. At the same time, I didn't want to know anything. The nausea of feeling so used, so heartlessly, kept hitting me. The bile in my throat kept surfacing unexpectedly.

Then there was also the realization that I couldn't live in this house. Not anymore. I had to move out, find a place I could afford, find a lawyer to represent me, and hold down a job while all this was happening. No way I wanted anybody at work to know what was going on.

Months passed in a haze, taking leave after leave on days I couldn't get myself out of bed. Ketki, my neighbour and only friend in Pune, would call to ask, 'All good?' What could I say? I said nothing.

I would keep standing numbly under the shower, letting the water wash over me. Then, again, I'd remember him, his touch, his skin on my skin. I'd rub my skin almost raw with the towel, harder, and harder to wipe out the distaste, the memory of his touch. Rub, rub, harder to get it out, out, out. It wouldn't leave.

It had been eighteen months since the day I got married. The lawyers' fees kept mounting. Then there was the cost of travel to Mumbai to attend hearings. I tried to get back my old job in Mumbai, but it had been filled. I even stayed away from my sister's wedding, the one person I loved more than anyone, because I couldn't bear facing any relatives.

I told my parents the bare minimum; even that shocked them to the core. Ranchi is still a small town, and the mothers could not bear to run into each other. I felt guilty about everything.

I had hit a new low. I had decided to quit my job. As luck had it, that day Ketki came over with some missal-pao she had made. I was overwhelmed that anyone even cared about me. It was the first time I broke down. Ketki gently probed why. I told her about what I had gone through and why I must leave Pune if I wanted to stay sane. Ketki looked shell-shocked. 'I would never have guessed looking at you,' she said. This surprised me. To me, my face was unrecognisable. Looking at myself in the mirror filled me with self-loathing.

Ketki suggested I try Japa Yoga, a mantra meditation practice which she found useful. She had talked about it earlier too, on our evening walks, but that was before this crisis. Now the thought of doing anything meditative, that would force me to confront my emotions, made me anxious. But not doing anything to face the endless questions in my head was even more frightening. I knew I had done nothing to be ashamed of, but I didn't think I could survive being left alone with my insecurities, my humiliation.

Ketki's reaction to my meltdown forced me to see myself through another person's eyes. I realised I couldn't get through this by myself. I finally gathered courage to face it. Found a centre that taught it. I told myself if it didn't work, I could always walk away. It wasn't as if everything became calm, like magic. It was tough to pull myself out of the sadness and self-pity. It was hard work. But it did work – slowly – acting like a vaccination shot. Somewhere in my head, I kept wishing I had done something like that when I was younger. My bullshit meter would have worked better.

Two years later, I was scraping the bottom in my bank account. The meditation training started giving me some inner strength, a lifeline I clung to, to face finding a new job. I wanted to make a clean start in a new city. Every time the destructive thoughts returned, of how I threw my career away and especially plaguing images of *them* together in bed – I would use Japa and my 108-beads mala and mantra to calm myself.

I considered moving to Gurgaon and making a new start. I couldn't think of asking Daddy to help pay the deposit on a room there. I knew they were already struggling on money. Every time I'd call him the guilt would swallow me up. To think that not long ago, I was the daughter who proudly sent her salary home.

I decided then to move back to familiar, but triggering, Mumbai. I started over, staying in the same girls' hostel as before – complete with its watery dal, old beds, the frustrating showers that ran dry mid-way. For a year, I depleted the last of my bank balance, going to interviews, taking any part-time job I could find – to survive from one month to the next. I lived this way until the lawyers' fees were paid and the divorce was finalised. Only then could I finally begin to rebuild my savings, a tiny safety net.

That ritual of bathing and wiping to remove every trace of his presence off my skin started to make me self-aware. I could see myself as if from a distance. Instead of self-pity, I had made the transition to anger. In a surreal way, I could view myself as I was then. So naïve, so eager to be loved. Sometimes I wished I could meet Prashant and slap the shit out of him.

I started to promise myself one thing. That if ever I had a second chance and I had a daughter – I was going to teach her to be selfish. Be selfish about everything. Why had no one taught me to value myself more? It is so important for women to be selfish. To not sublimate everything we have striven for – our careers, our dreams, our desires – to just take second place to someone. No one teaches women to be selfish. To say no to a lover or an employer or even a parent from always expecting more from you. Why? Just because you are a girl? The anger, betrayal, even waves of self-pity do come back to overwhelm me sometimes. But less frequently. I'm teaching myself to view these emotions with more compassion for myself.

I think if I hadn't been introduced to the calming Japa practice, I would have wanted to inflict pain on the two bastards. For using me so cold-heartedly as the cover for their relationship. Earlier, I was critical of all that I felt was wrong with me. My hair – too frizzy; my lips – too big, I used to feel then. I like my body and myself a little better now, after all this. That I could survive those destructive rejections, the cold remarks he would make. That I could rebuild myself, and not become a trembling mess anytime anyone who didn't know that I was now divorced would bring up his name.

I am more aware of my triggers now and walk away from such situations.

I read somewhere that only 11 per cent of people in the world are born with curly hair. I'm in a minority and it's taken me all these years and painful processing to appreciate myself. I've honestly grown to love my hair. People would pay to have curls like mine. I wear my hair long and open. Initially, I saw it as a protective halo. Lately I've started seeing it as a frame to myself, to this work in progress.

Call it selfishness or call it self-preservation. As far as I'm concerned, they are the two positive things I have learned from this experience.

3

It's negative appraisal time: Of your ex and what you had

∞

I know you're thinking it's easy to say 'choose yourself'. Especially when your feelings aren't fading. Tell me something – isn't your mind still stuck, selectively remembering the good parts? It's like it glossed over the hurtful memories and painted an unreal picture from nostalgia. My goal is to help you keep it real and come out of this phase, feeling more sorted.

There's more to getting over someone than just waiting it out. A study found that *focusing on the stuff that wasn't great about your ex* or the relationship can actually help you get some perspective back.

It's time to do a negative appraisal.

This involves making note of the unpleasant things about your ex and the relationship. You might think 'that feels mean' or 'that's not how I am'. But your brain has probably already been exaggerating all the good stuff and created a new imbalance in your memory. So doing a negative appraisal of the ex will actually correct the distortion.

We tend to remember the fun moments, the sweet milestones, etc but *what about the compromises you had to make? The times you felt unheard or frustrated? Those things were real too.* Consciously remind yourself of your ex's annoying habits, the triggers for arguments, times you felt unacknowledged, the double standards, or things that just didn't work for you as a couple. They all added up to the disenchantment. Like maybe you were a social person, he was not; and it became a source of friction; or that he would never introduce you to his work friends; or made negative comments about anyone *you* introduced them to. Add it into your journal.

Think of it as an old-fashioned report card. You are your toughest teacher.

When I was a kid, report cards were brutal. Teachers could go on and on about all that was wrong with you. There was none of the glowing praise you see nowadays, when it seems like every kid ever born comes out smelling like roses; a prodigy in the making. My teachers called a spade a spade, sparing nothing at all, in the mission to keep you humble! I have spent my life being told 'Lacks concentration,' often in harsher words than that.

This is what you need to do. Think of the most heartless teacher or boss you've had, who never minced their words. Mine was a lady called Pandit. *Today you are going to be the Pandit of your life.* You will cast a brutal eye over all that happened – as if my thorny-mouthed Pandit or your toughest teacher or boss is reading your story. They would call out the fake shit, all the red flags that were waving in your face, but which you chose to ignore. I was once given to moping around over a man who would drive away after a fight, who never came back to apologise, while I stood Juliet-style on my balcony for hours, hoping that anytime now I would hear his bike return. Morning would arrive but he would not. I can imagine what Pandit may have said in that sharp voice of hers. 'Thappad lagaoon ek aake?' (Shall I come give you a tight slap?)

Your work is to get over that person. And no, do not try justifying them or the reasons for their behaviour to yourself or to me. What you are going through, as a result of whatever happened, is all I care about. So bring your focus to read the examples I've given below of red flags. Reminder: I hope you've written your heartbreak notes, because I'll ask you to refer to them after this. (You really better have written it, or else '*Thappad lagaoon ek aake?*')

Red flags you should have seen then. Get wise now.

1. Extreme jealousy: Not cute. Love doesn't confer ownership.

People are not your possessions. Genuine love can't be about trying to own someone. It is about liking another person for who they are. Did you ever feel like you were under scrutiny in your relationship? Did your ex. interrogate you about your social life or have negative feelings about your time apart? Attitudes like that often lead to hurt and misunderstanding because they are not built on a foundation of equality and care. My friend's boyfriend was once deeply upset and *pretttty* nasty because she wasn't home at a time he 'expected' her to be there. Our gang had taken off straight after college; to celebrate someone's birthday and she didn't think to keep him informed. This was way before we had mobile phones. He got nasty with her about forgetting to tell *her parents to tell him.* (She wasn't allowed to call up his home.) Not funny! It showed his proprietorial attitude and continued right through their relationship. My friend saw the early signs of his entitled anger at being deprived of what he saw as 'his time'. She wishes to this day she had called out the behaviour right then, or walked away in time.

2. Controlling behaviour: It's not love. It's a desire to manipulate and dominate.

A partner who attempts to dominate your life by dictating things like who you hang out with, where you go, what work you do, where you holiday, how *you* use *your* money or who you can/cannot talk to, etc. isn't just being involved. Often, it's only the beginning of more control. I know many people whose partners have problems with their choice of clothes. (Read Vani's story, 'Power games'.) Seriously. *Anyone who oversteps boundaries,* trying to control anything that is part of who you are, whether it is about your personality; what you want to do, including professional choices; who doesn't think twice about making decisions on your behalf *is not thinking of you in all that. They are trying to manipulate you to fit into their mould of who they think you should be.* If a partner intrudes on your privacy, monitors your phone or social media – it's a clear warning, pointing to potentially dangerous patterns. If your ex showed any such signs of being dominating, *be glad it ended* between you both.

3. Inconsistency, evasiveness: It comes down to trust.

While a degree of mystery can add excitement to a

relationship, excessive secrecy is worrying. It points to untrustworthiness and a lack of commitment. Who wants to be in a place where you feel that your partner is hiding something? The goal has to be good communication. Unless the person you're involved with works for some super-secret mission – then by all means deal with things on a need-to-know basis. But that's rare! For the rest of us ordinary mortals, secrecy that becomes borderline paranoia should raise your antennae: things like hiding texts, emails, not being open about who they are with or where they are, consistently giving vague, evasive answers to reasonable questions. If you had clearly expressed your concerns and even then, after a reasonable time, you found the person continuing to vault their secret 'other' life on their devices, there seems a strong chance, she/he thought they were getting away with it. Consider yourself lucky you're out of this person's radius.

4. Emotional issues: Debunk stereotypes. Communicate. Of course, people express their feelings differently. No one has to conform to a standard, and definitely not to a gender stereotype like 'guys must be tough, guys can't show their vulnerability'. Your heartbreak notes (write them already!) will have shown you what your ex's EQ (emotional quotient) was like. For example, some people may appear emotionally distant, while others might suppress anger until it erupts. Look at how your ex/former partner expressed their emotions. Overall, was it balanced? Were there over-the-top outbursts or sullen moods? This will have impacted your relationship and your own sense of emotional safety. It would have directly affected how they treated you. Unhealthy emotional expression like yelling at you or others, walking away and cooling off and returning after long periods of not replying to your communication can screw up the relationship's dynamic. It raises a big red flag about how they handle conflict.

5. Name-calling: Call it out. Or cut loose.

Did your relationship have times when your ex would use derogatory words to put you down? Words like crazy, dumb, bitch, fuckwit, brainless, ugly, fat, choot lazy, cow cunt or any other demeaning word or phrase?

IT IS NOT OK. NEVER. Yes, disagreements are normal in any relationship. And people should be able to express their hurt or unhappiness over the other person's behaviour. But it cannot ever become personal. Not about the person or their friends and family. Any argument should be about the behaviour or how it made you feel, but it cannot attack or insult a person or their character. If it had started happening in your relationship, have no doubt it would only have grown. Name-calling is just unacceptable. There are no two ways about it. Any instances of that in your heartbreak notes? Underline and highlight them.

6. Silent treatment: Pure manipulation.

Taking a break during a heated argument to cool down can be healthy, with clear communication about intent. Like, 'I'm coming back, okay? Let's figure it out.' There's a huge difference between that and someone who constantly gives you the silent treatment. A cold war can become a manipulative tactic to punish or control. When one partner unilaterally decides how long the impasse must last, ignores the other person's attempts to reconnect, and only they decide when the conflict is over – it leaves the other person feeling powerless. This is a massive red flag. An aunt and uncle's cold wars were well-known in our family. They could keep it going for weeks sometimes, with only terse words shot at each other, the bare minimum needed to coordinate their lives. I used to wonder how those cold wars ended and what kind of damage they did.

7. Lack of accountability: The 'who, me?' 'Not me!' person

People who refuse to own their decisions or take accountability will always be trying to fix blame on someone else. This kind of behaviour is usually a cover for someone who basically avoids facing up to their shortcomings. You'd also often have seen them pushing problems into the background, letting them fester. Please understand. It is not *all* your fault. If they say it is, and try to make you feel guilty when you know you aren't – hello! That's a person with a 'blame-game' and 'maine kya kiya': (what did I do?) kind of avoidant mindset. Major red flag alert! Communicate, seek therapy. Or face bigger issues later.

8. Boundaries: The 'so what if I did that' person

Boundaries are important in every relationship – whether it's parent and child, boss and employee, siblings, close friends. And it is especially important between you and the love of your life. Someone who repeatedly oversteps boundaries is a legit red flag. Let's say you met someone for a few dates, they were good ones, now you decide to go to their apartment. There you find that they are pressuring you to do stuff you don't want to do. Or imagine you come back from the loo, and find them looking at your phone. Or that a food delivery arrived, and you come in from the balcony to see them looking through your stuff. It's irrelevant whether the phone is or isn't password protected. The point is that they overstepped a boundary; they did it without checking if it was okay by you. It shows disrespect for you, and can easily cross into more violations of your trust.

9. Constant comparison to an ex is a big-time reason for bye-bye time.

I don't want to be someone else and no one else can be me. It's true for each of us! Comparison is a killjoy. When has it ever left you feeling good? Not when a parent compared you with your sibling, a teacher brought you down vis-a-vis their blue-eyed student, or a boss pitted you against your colleagues. I mean, if you were training for a sport and your coach sees comparison as a way to push you to up your game, that's between you and the coach. But if your partner compares you with their previous partners, that person is just equal to a low-life, in my opinion. *I only want a partner who thinks I'm fantastic in an absolute way. Not in a greater than or lesser than so-and-so way.* If a partner compares you with some random ex or exes, what does that even suggest? That this person thinks you do not measure up, or that you are okaaaay kinda, sorta, but someone else is better? Hey, enough people did enough damage in keeping our self-esteem six feet under. Do we actually want anyone else, who is not even related by blood, to do that to us again? I didn't think so.

See Red. Get angry. Get the message!

They are called red flags for good reason. The colour RED universally stands for danger, warning. It means STOP. STOP drowning in your misery. STOP self-sabotaging. STOP worrying about being alone. Recognise how close you were to losing yourself in that whole shit show!

You are alive right now. Let go. Letting go isn't a sign of weakness. It takes strength to pull yourself out of your pain. To believe that you deserve better. Next time, recognise that red means STOP.

After night comes dawn. After red will come green.

In Buddhism, they say that 'winter always turns to spring.' It is the law of nature, of life. Suffering is no exception. It will ease. Every red traffic light is not the same, is it? Some red lights turn to green faster, some take longer, but turn to green they will. You too will see things change for yourself. The right kind of love, and person, the kind that fights *for* you, not against you, will happen. How can I say this? Because *your personal manifesto is your promise to yourself to be that person who will not settle* for anything less. You *will come out wiser* after this experience and know what standards you demand from life. There *will* come a time when you meet someone whose behaviour show you genuineness, whose attraction to you isn't only physical, but also to your mind and soul. Someone who follows through on what they say they'll do, who is kind to others. Someone who is genuinely curious about you, your life, your interests, your past; who listens and remembers details later. They respond promptly (let's not get unreasonable about it though), are clear about their availability, and don't play games. They respect your 'no' and your boundaries without argument. They are consistent and do what they say they will.

Your self-talk has to change to seeing yourself doing well on all the fronts that matter to you. And in that, if you wish, also see a partner who roots for you and celebrates your wins.

The negative appraisal

EXIT THE HEARTBREAK
EXamine

Step 1: Pull out your heartbreak notes for reference.
Step 2: Get yourself a red pen and red/orange highlighters. If you made the journal on a digital file, you will still need some paper/pens to do this.
Step 3: Think of your toughest, zero-bullshit-tolerance teacher or boss. Imagine you are that teacher/boss right now.
Step 4: Run through the incidents in the diary. Look at them critically with a clear head. Keep underlining with a red pen all the times their behaviour was not okay. Liberally add exclamation marks where needed!

(Write in the margin if you wish, just as your teacher did. A one-word comment is fine but be absolutely objective in this. Comments can be things like: 'Kept quiet when xyz made nasty jokes at my expense.' See what their actions should have alerted you to. Be fair. A one-off slip up that was never repeated may not necessarily have been a red flag. But please do not go soft on the negative appraisal.)
Step 5: Do not overlook or brush away something that you know left you uncomfortable or unhappy. Not all red flags come out in the open as blazing red flags. They sometimes come disguised as a big bunch of red roses *after a stomach-churning disagreement* (without the conversation or understanding that you wanted). Or a bunch of red-kissy-lips emoticons in a text message – *after*

they didn't reply for two days! And you know how badly that messed with your head.

If you're seeing lots of red, get the message. They are not worth your tears.

Slow burn: Manoj's story

∞

Shikha and I had known each other a long time. We even played pithhoo as kids. Our houses were in Maninagar, Ahmedabad; in a lane with a lot of Marwaris. I was in an all-boys school. She was in an all-girls school. I wasn't keen on studies. I've always been really big on movies. Shikha was studying engineering. Her only reading was academic. We gravitated towards each other because unlike other Marwari kids, we weren't wired to be business people. My dreams were simpler than hers. I just knew I liked films a lot, with no idea what to do with that. I never thought I could be with any girl, let alone this kind of studious girl. We started hanging out more and more. The neighbourhood knew. The parents knew. Nobody created issues. Our closeness built up slowly with babyish stuff like exchanging glances, walking down the street together, having meals at each other's houses. No sleepovers. That wasn't done in our community. Moreover, I like the morning thing, she did the late-night thing. My mom-dad had a five-year age gap; her parents had a seven-year age gap, so her being two years older than me didn't matter either. We were both probably a bit oblivious, while everyone else knew where we were headed. Shikha had anger spells. Only I could calm her down. For seven years, we dated. There were stolen kisses, cuddles, but physically nothing happened till I was maybe twenty-two.

I was obsessed with cinema, downloading more and more. She was fixated on wanting more and more – of sex. Even our first time together was on her encouragement. I was fine to wait till we formalised our relationship. She didn't think that was important. We reached a stage of once-a-month sex when her parents went to visit her Dada-Dadi. I wasn't willing to risk going and doing it stupidly somewhere. Once we were in a movie hall, and she started playing with me. I froze. Anyone we know could have seen us. I hissed, 'Why the burning hurry? Don't be foolish.' She was furious. Wouldn't even let me explain properly that we had our whole life to have fun, safely, later.

Somewhere around this time she applied for a student exchange programme abroad. There she met a guy – Rishi, also an *Amdavadi* (connected with Ahmedabad). Apparently, they got pretty close over there. I thought he was a casual friend who she talked about. We weren't a sticky, clingy couple, the kind that try to keep tabs on each other. In any case, I was busy prepping for my final exams and would say 'Leave me alone for three days, I have to study.' She started using the time to meet that Rishi. When my results came out, they weren't great. My father also started keeping unwell. I decided to ditch doing my master's and join the family business.

By now she'd finished her engineering and was interning with a company. Our parents trusted us. We'd even set an engagement date. On Diwali, we planned a party at her house. She'd call her friends, I'd call mine. She had barely mentioned Rishi till then, but now she said she'd be calling him as well. I had no reason for doubt at all. All the women in my life, even the neighbourhood Maadu aunties, knew that Manoj was serious about Shikha. At family weddings everyone knew her and loved her. We never argued over anything; the maximum we argued was over food. She was health-conscious. I am very fond of rich Maadu food and would rather risk being unhealthy than deny myself that pleasure.

Since it was Diwali, everyone insisted we play teen patti. After many rounds, we took a break. I'm the more social one between us. I was happily chatting with friends on the balcony. Maybe 30-40 minutes later, I realised I hadn't seen Shikha around. Vaguely, I noticed that Rishi, the guy from her course, was also missing. I went to her room. It was locked. I had the key to it. I was thinking I'll get my spare house-key which is kept in her room. I unlocked the room, opened the door, and found them both inside. Fully naked. In the middle of sex. I got mind-fucked. She was looking at me. I closed the door. I left the key in the lock. I took a cab to the Sabarmati riverfront. I've always felt so much calm there, in Gandhiji's special place, this one place that stands for truth. But it was closed already. I asked the cab driver to take me to Atal bridge. I needed to just look out on the water, and stop the waves of shock that were washing over me.

Cry? No. I wasn't that kind of person. Question her? No. *Pooch ke kya milega?* (What would I know by asking her?) I never went on to ask her. I kept feeling – One, what am I going to do? I have seen this now. Two, I am not taking her back. She cheated. Three, I'll have to tell my parents.

I felt hopeless.

What do I do now, I kept thinking? All I remember of that Diwali night, standing at Atal bridge, which was probably lit up in all its neon colours with its laser lights reflecting on the water, was that I could only see the water stretching endlessly, black. Its liquid witchery slithered – sinister, dark, snakelike and sad. It was the darkest night on this day of the festival of lights.

I pulled myself away. Went home. My parents were out of town to celebrate Diwali with my Dada-Dadi. My father had suggested I ask Shikha to do the office mahurat, since we were almost 'official'. I lied, got my sister only to do it. I started thinking what's the point of all this healthy eating. I'd stuff myself even more. It took me a month to tell Dad that Shikha and I have decided to part.

She never tried to contact me even once and I didn't ask her anything either. Shikha went around telling everyone it was over. Left me to try and handle that question '*Kya hua?*' (What happened?) A mutual friend bumped into me at an engagement. Again, he asked, 'Kya hua?'

Shikha knew fully well I was too much of a gentleman to tell people what actually happened. Maybe she thought she'll push me into confronting her; to tell me I was too boring and she wanted more excitement from life. I kept telling myself good riddance, but part of me couldn't forget her expression when I had opened the door. My face would go red, thinking what a fool she had made of me.

On my birthday she tried calling me. I thought

maybe we can be friends. After all, being with her was seven years of my life. I picked up the phone but then she started crying. I couldn't take it. I couldn't bear the sound of her crying or get past what had happened. I threw myself more into my dad's business.

One day, out of the blue, my mother comes and says, 'Manoj, I can see how miserable you are. Whatever has happened, beta, give her a chance.' I had no idea where that came from. How could I tell her what happened? Finally, when my best friend confronted me again, I told him. He was in shock too. He kept saying, 'It's sick, man, sick, that she was sleeping with both of you at the same time.'

It didn't hit me then. But it hit me later, in phases, that she'd been sleeping with that Rishi when she went abroad and when I was busy studying. All along.

At my cousin's wedding, everybody was rehearsing for performances, dancing, drinking. I saw myself, the sad, lonely guy at the bar. I used to be so trustful. I'd become wary now. If a friend set me up for a casual date, I'd ask the woman too many personal questions. I kept replaying that Diwali night. Rewind, forward, rewind, forward, play. Her picking that guy to be on her teen patti team. That guy clinging to her. Me, sitting there innocently, oblivious, assuming he was stuck to her because he didn't know others at the party. It never occurred to me that he was fucking my girlfriend right under my nose.

I am not looking out for women at all. I could see the spark between my cousin and his wife-to-be at their wedding. It hit me again that by now I could have been married. So much happened after that. Demonetization hit my father's business hugely. I lost interest in it all. I decided to get a job. After eight months of chasing all kinds of leads, with just a BA degree, I got a job as course coordinator at a media school. They have film studies as one of the master's programmes. I told my dad that he can start shutting down the business, I will earn enough for our family to manage. I've also signed up for an MA in Film Studies in an executive programme which I can do part time, with evening classes.

Shikha still lives two houses away from me. I told dad – there's no need to move homes because of this fiasco. This year, she called again on my birthday to explain why it happened. 'I needed more sex.' Fine, I get that she was a more physical person than me. It sounds strange, I know, that a boy doesn't want to have sex as much as the girl does. But she couldn't understand my thinking. In our kind of families, every action you take needs to build trust.

We bump into each other. We exchange hi's and byes. We have blocked each other on social media. I deleted her number too but didn't block it. She is an engineer, with a big company, the hot-shot woman in the neighbourhood. Sometimes I think I should forgive, get over it, add her number back on my phone. That guy meant nothing to her. I heard their scene ended that night itself. He was a *hawa ka jhoka* (fleeting wind) in our life, *kab aaya kab gaya* (Who knows when it came and when it went) but he blew a storm that I'm still recovering from.

One happy development: I started a film club at the

media centre where I work. I got permission to use their resources and host a once-a-month film discussion. I'm clear that the purpose of this club must only be the love for films. Nothing else. We meet, have a passionate discussion about a film. Then we all take our buses and metros and go home. If women ask me out from the film club – it's happened once or twice – I don't go down that road. I tell myself I'm not looking for love. After Shikha, I feel like I went back to my oldest love, even older than my love for her – cinema. My mind and heart have wiped out the Shikha years in my life. I don't go out seeking anyone even if I may possibly be the only last single guy I know. Ok, qualifier, the last single 30-year-old Maadu guy I know.

Maybe it will change, maybe it won't. The time I'm taking to recover fully is going to be an even slower burn than the way I fell in love. I have never been a man in a hurry and now it's even more so.

Just vibing: Shubra's story

I was new to dating apps and stunned that anyone I swiped right on was a match. This, despite the fact that I hadn't put up any pics of my face on my profile, just sensuous pics of my neck and hands. The thing is, I'm a married woman. I teach physics at one of the biggest colleges in Udaipur and don't want to be recognised.

Ajay, my husband, developed erectile dysfunction in the fifth year of our marriage. No one could say why exactly. Plus, he was closed to finding other ways to be intimate. What he called his bad luck, I saw as our destiny. I had decided I wouldn't walk away from it. My husband suggested we have separate bedrooms. He said my early start to get to college disturbed him and I was relieved not to have to suffer the failed attempts at intimacy.

It took me 25 years of self-pity to wake up from a sexless marriage, step out of my prison of fidelity and try and find myself love. The catch was I still really did want love, not just sex. But guys on dating apps were only interested in a 'hook up' – a phrase I had only just learnt.

Then this profile called 'JV–Just Vibing' started giving me good vibes. He was in no hurry to take it to WhatsApp or to meet. My profile name was 'Shh' (short for my real name Shubra and for the way I wanted it to be – quiet). I was transparent in my write-up that I was married but looking for a long-term relationship. JV told me that he was separated from his wife; that he had a kid in middle school. So clearly, he was much younger than me. My son was almost 25. I had him soon after getting married.

JV and I (as Shh) chatted on the app for a month or two before we took it to WhatsApp. I loved the links he shared – sublime music, beautiful passages from books. His texts just lit me up. I think his best move was to let me hunger for a move from him. I couldn't wait to hear his voice. Finally, I only called him up one night.

JV had told me that he and his wife were also separated. Later I understood, he meant they lived in separate rooms in the same house. Both of them had been apolitical in the beginning, but a difficult pregnancy on bed rest and too much time on her phone led her down online rabbit holes. Next thing he knew, she was trying to convert him to her newfound political dogmas. It led to massive disagreements. I felt for him. We were both stuck in unhappy marriages we couldn't walk away from.

Quite early on, I had texted him, 'I don't even know your real name. And what do you do?' He asked, "Why?'

I said, 'No reason, anything is fine, but I hope you aren't a poet.'

I swear it felt like there was a missed beat. After a while, he replied, 'Sorry koi call thha. But why? What have poets done to you?' I said, 'I'd rather not talk about it, OK?' He changed the topic immediately. I didn't want to dwell on Raveen, the first guy I had been involved with, way before I met my husband. I had fallen like a ton of bricks for his charm, intellect, chiselled features and smooth sher-o-shairi that rolled off his tongue in a low, sensuous drawl. I had imagined our future, even children with poetic names and long lashes like his. I was shattered the day I realised he was playing more women like me. It took me a long time to recover. So, a poet was a no-no in my head. Two months later, I realised JV was one too. He could have risked telling me the truth. That he was Aman, a struggling lyricist with a day job in accounts. Maybe I'd have called it off. He gambled. And it paid off. I was already in too deep.

We had taken to meeting at my friend's vacant apartment. I would get there early, clean the whole place, carry every damn thing to make the love-nest cozy. I'd be dropping off to sleep by the time he'd reach. But then he'd kiss me and I'd be like white chocolate melting in his big, brown, clean-smelling arms.

JV (I still called him that) just had to hold me, say 'Shh....kaisi ho?' (Shh...how are you?), and I could forgive him anything: his reaching late, his almost always being broke. He was going through a bad time. I didn't mind paying for things sometimes, like his Uber ride. The first time we spent a whole night together, I was astounded at how often he could want to do it. He called it 'Duracelling,' after the ad where the Duracell bunny on those batteries just goes on and on and on. Starved as I was, of touch and affection, this was very new. Finally, my body felt awake, my heart sang – from being desired, from the afterglow of lying entwined with a man I couldn't stop thinking about. He said if his wife knew he was busy Duracelling with someone, it would be over. He couldn't put his kid through that.

I would be giggling all day in my college. Me, a no-nonsense physics teacher with a sudden love for chemistry. And what chemistry we had! Every single time we met, the bliss of just lying together, sweaty and spent, was unbelievable. I started imagining this was going to be my maybe-not-perfect-but-perfect-enough forever relationship.

One time as we lay together, I mentioned being exclusive. I couldn't even have thought he'd want it any different. I also said something about my son getting married soon. I wanted JV to be at the wedding; to see me all prettied up. I thought I'd pass JV off as my gym friend. He headed to the loo like he hadn't heard me and started showering. I went over what I had said. What part of it could have got him uptight? I was sure he had heard me.

I asked him to just be upfront. Instead, he started teasing me, 'Arre wah, you're going to become a M. I. L!' I quipped back, 'Hey. I'm going to be a M.I.L.F.' He continued joking, 'Good one. Add it to your dating app intro. You'll have guys swarming around you like flies.'

'What the fuck are you saying?' I snapped at him. 'Let's leave.' We had got into a habit where he would drive my car almost up to my house and then he'd Uber it back to his place. It was the sweetest part, playing music, taking longer routes, like we were a couple. That day we drove in silence. I held back my tears. He said, 'What's all this sudden talk about being exclusive? There are so many beautiful people out there in the dating world. Why not experience all that?'

I tersely replied, 'I told you from the start what I was looking for. Did I say I wanted an open relationship?' He snapped, 'You get so intense. For fuck's sake, I'm joking.' Then, like I was a tantrummy child, he said, 'C'mon, gimme a smile.' And I did. It was a weak, sad one; it still makes me sick that I did it.

I kept going over that conversation. Like what did my age have to do with anything, especially if he had feelings for me, which surely, he did. I knew that pretty early on I'd said that I wanted a monogamous relationship. Everything felt fuzzy.

I started to feel angry at everything; that my son had chosen to marry so young, that I was old, that my life was wasted, that had I met JV earlier, it might have turned out differently. The frequency and tone of his texts changed. Unfortunately, my feelings didn't.

I was desperate to see him again. Part of me hoped that if we were together just once more; if he kissed me, everything would go back to the way it was.

Two weeks before my son's wedding, I got the keys to my friend's apartment. I sent JV a pic of the key and a text with the date and time. He replied with a heart emoticon. Our code for 'confirmed'. I took care to dress nicely, drove all the way to the apartment, and waited. He never showed up.

I struggled to act normal while doing all the wedding prep. Right through the wedding events I was snappy and on the edge of hysteria all the time. Everyone thought it was the wedding stress.

His texts didn't stop. They just became more non-committal. Now anyone could have read our chat history and assumed it was just two casual friends. I had nobody to talk to except for my friend Bindiya who knew everything, whose apartment keys I would borrow. I was often in a pathetic state by 3:00 a.m., and she was the only one I would keep reaching out to. She's a dynamic, divorced, sorted woman – very clear about the role of men in her life. So often she'd told me 'Give less importance to your personal relationships and throw yourself into your work. Have you ever thought of doing your PhD, Shubi?'

What can I say? I was so ashamed of being made a fool of, and what a fool I'd made of myself.

Bindiya suggested I go back on the dating apps. 'Look at it as therapy,' she said, since I was resisting therapy. So, I created a new profile for myself on the dating apps. This time I didn't put up any clever pics. Just a meme. And the profile name 'IYKYK' (If You Know You Know). That was it.

I started flipping through the profiles, left, left, left… my heart just wasn't in it. Then I stopped suddenly. I saw the same 'Just Vibing' meme that was on JV's profile pic when I had swiped right on him. I told myself it could be a coincidence. I swiped right to see what happens. In minutes, it was a match. I waited. The opening chat was one of his favourite memes.

Now here's where it gets more shitty. While he was clearly waiting for a reply from 'IYKYK (my new dating profile name), he messages me, Shubra, on my WhatsApp. 'Hey Shh…kaisi ho?'

I started texting my best friend Bindiya in a panic. 'What audacity! Should I unmatch?'

Bindiya said, 'Keep texting as IYKYK. I'll tell you what to say.' So, in a very unlike-me way, I started texting. Here's the thing. I, Shubhra have always responded fast to JV, even now; but IYKYK took her sweet time to reply. She was self-assured, and cutting as hell. I kept texting whatever Bindiya told me, to see where it goes. JV was eager to meet IYKYK that very evening. She agreed to meet; she controlled the narrative and picked a location very far from where he was – at a cafe near the airport. He begged for a meeting point somewhere closer. IYKYK refused to bend. 'Take it or leave it, lover,' she said firmly. She said, 'Are you even worth my time? I don't want to meet you and then discover you're a fucking 4-inch man-child.'

I kept texting JV as IYKYK. The shameless skirt-chaser agreed to all of her demands. IYKYK told him to pick a nice five-star hotel in the area. 'This is where we'll go, after we meet at the cafe. Provided you don't put me off. You understand you can't take that for granted?'

I was practically peeing my pants texting all this as IYKYK to JV. Between the texts, he kept sending me, the real Shubra, general chitchat on his job search. I was going out of my mind between texting him, sharing his dating app texts with Bindiya, and copy-pasting her smart-ass replies to JV.

The meeting was set for 7:00 p.m.

I debated with Bindiya if I should land up there and confront him. 'Up to you, Shubi,' she said. 'I'm off for an event. Tell me later kya hua.'

I decided to keep in touch as IYKYK on the dating app, till he had driven an hour and a half, reaching the cafe fifteen minutes late. Of course, he got there and saw no one. No IYKYK, in fact no one there at all. As luck would have it, that cafe had shut down. He kept texting, puzzled by the no-show. I unleashed all my pent-up anger against the lying, ageist asshole.

As IYKYK, I gave it to him. 'You call me to a place that's been shut down and think I'll wait around for you? Go drive back to your pathetic life, in some loser job.' I was hitting him where I knew it would hurt the most. The texts from JV still kept coming. 'Come on, I had no idea the place had closed.' (To be honest, I didn't either, that was a stroke of luck.) 'Do you know how long it's taken me to reach here? Where are you? Let's begin again.'

I went quiet on him this time. The dude who had chronically been too broke to buy fuel to drive up to meet me, suddenly had money to go all that distance to meet an unknown woman – for the thrill of a new adventure.

It was just the splash of ice-cold water that I needed.

He still sends me/Shubra forwards. I respond sometimes with emoticons, but my heart is all cried out and stronger now. Now and then, he sends me a piece of music that tugs at my heartstrings, and almost brings me to tears again. But he must never know. Just vibing is not for me. I know better now. I have Better Vibes in my life.

It's a vibe alright; I tell you. A very discreet one. More reliable than men. It doesn't mess with my head or interfere with my PhD study. It knows its rightful place in my life. In a corner of my bedside drawer.

4

This is a lot more about you, than about them

I was fortunate to find a really good mental health counsellor almost 25 years ago who helped me work through some of my childhood trauma. She helped me see how I had pushed away my unacknowledged issues into the deep recesses of my mind. I realised that for baby Milan, it was the only way to cope and carry on. Years later, when I lost my beloved father, I struggled to deal with the incomprehensible loss. The worst part was that I seemed to have lost all my memories of him, the big, small, simple, everyday ones even – on losing him. My counsellor made a reference to our long-ago discussion about my childhood traumas. I was pretty exasperated and said, 'Oh, come on! What does that have to do with this? Can we not link everything back to bloody childhood?' She asked me to hear her out and reminded me of the coping mechanism I had used as a child. Which was to block whatever was too much to handle. She helped me make the connection that the coping mechanism I was using to deal with the grief of losing my father was exactly what I had used as a child to block trauma. I realised then that as much as we may pooh pooh all those who think everything can't be linked to childhood, the truth is, almost everything *is actually* connected.

Childhood trauma can and will shape your attachment style

According to psychologists John Bowlby and Mary Ainsworth, every infant needs one really solid, loving relationship with at least one primary caregiver, so that he or she can effectively learn to manage their feelings later in life, in intimate relationships. This is not to say our parents are to blame for everything. I'm serious about this. This is not about attaching blame but finding understanding, so we can heal and trust again. Our parents did the best they knew. But how *we felt, how that little child within us felt,* and what Baby Milan (add your name here, Baby You) learned of love in childhood – that is what we carry into our adult relationships. Early life experiences, including trauma, influence the attachment styles we develop big time. Trauma is a heavy word, right? But it doesn't have to be extreme like some life-changing event. It can be even in the overall environment we grew up in. For example, maybe Baby You grew up in a chaotic or neglectful environment. Maybe 'Baby You' learnt that your needs would not be met consistently. You then struggled to trust that others would be reliable and responsive to your needs. That's one kind of trauma. There can be many others. Having caregivers who are consistently dysregulated, a home where there is abuse (verbal, physical, mental, sexual, any kind), differentiation between genders, neglect, violence, narcissism, chaos, or inconsistently met needs –

any of that trauma, whether it was in childhood or later, leaves attachment wounds. All trauma can contribute to insecure attachment patterns.

'Attachment wounds' and how they shape our attachment styles

Basically, when you are attached to someone like a parent or caregiver, but your attachment needs are not met as a child, this lack, this gaping need majorly affects how you see yourself and others. It could even be later, like with a partner early in life. It impacts how you deal with your emotions and how you form relationships. It directly influences your self-talk, your emotions, and how you try to achieve emotional safety.

Attachment style is the way Adult-You tries to cope with what Baby-You went through.

There are four attachment styles, of which, one is secure and three are insecure styles. First, the secure lot. These lucky souls, who had a nurturing relationship with their caregiver, grew up feeling worthy and lovable. People with a secure attachment style can handle intimacy along with the uncertainty that comes with it. They often gravitate to securely-attached people. Then there are those with insecure attachment styles. These are people with anxious-preoccupied, dismissive-avoidant and fearful-avoidant attachment styles. The good news is that it's possible to have a secure-attachment style even if you experienced some form of trauma. That's the holy grail, if you ask me – to reach that point of self-knowledge and sense of security.

What is your attachment style? Know it to work on it.

You can say, 'why do I need this? I'm fine. I'm not broken.' Every failed relationship, every text you wait for, every call that goes unanswered is a reminder that the emotional wound inside you needs to be seen to. The anxious pull you feel, the fear of being left like this, *it is not about them. It is about what was missing long before they entered your life.* The love you didn't receive. The safety you never felt. And the validation you learned to beg for or run away from, because asking for it wasn't safe.

In Trixie's true story, 'February 13th, 14th or 15th', we read how she always made the first move by sending the same meme to every person she matched with. The varied responses made it such an eye-opener to her about the unseen person at the other end. I've often thought how fascinating it is, that the same stimulus can lead to such different responses in people. The *same kind of stimulus and trauma may lead to different attachment styles* in different individuals. While attachment styles are not written in stone, they do help in understanding ourselves and other people better. See if you recognise yourself and your ex in any of these.

Anxious attachment: A person with an anxious attachment style has trouble trusting others. They often become dependent or clingy, even possessive, constantly seeking reassurance in their relationships. They seem to have a fear of abandonment. Anxious attached people might have had a pattern of texting their parent (when young) and their romantic partner (later in life) many times. They are often self-blaming and can become controlling in a relationship. They're good at noticing shifts in others' emotions and quick to comfort someone who is crying. They want to feel close to others but their fear of abandonment and trust issues can get in the way of true intimacy. It can be exhausting. The chasing? That's the anxious attached person's inner child crying out, 'Please see me. Please love me. Please don't leave me.'

The love you're chasing in your romantic relationships can't replace the loss you've been avoiding. Still, you don't need to be stuck in the anxious attached groove. It'll need conscious work, preferably with a therapist, to develop a more secure attachment style.

Avoidant attachment: A person with an avoidant attachment style has a predominant fear of loss, because of early childhood experiences, which they mask as independence. They also reduce their own needs for connection, find it difficult to trust themselves or others and quite often have a negative self-image. Their behaviour might look like an unwillingness to commit to a relationship, being too picky about another's habits, keeping secrets and avoiding sharing much about themselves. They might even seem distant. For example, if you ask how their day was, they will answer with one word like 'fine'.

Avoidant attached people might have trouble being emotionally available to others as they fear getting too close. The avoidant-attached person is prone to withdraw from others, become more isolated, dissociative or angry. They tend to avoid any close, intimate relationship. The prospect of a partner who could become dependent frightens them. Avoidant-attached people will often have faced trauma related to neglect. And that's why they fear getting too close to others and have a high need for self-protection, to keep themselves emotionally safe. Avoidants need to seek support on these issues to learn to trust others.

The avoidant attached person's reactions are almost diametrically opposite to the anxious attached person's. While the anxious attached person becomes clingy in their need, the avoidant attached person wants to detach and escape commitment. A relationship between two people like that is almost a recipe for heartbreak, unless there is awareness and communication.

Disorganised avoidant attachment: Then there's a combined or confused attachment style. An anxious/ fearful disorganised avoidant attachment style. Think of it as a person on a mental see-saw. These people battle internally between anxious and avoidant tendencies. They want closeness but once it's there, they get overwhelmed and tend to push others away. They can swing between a cycle of nearness and distance without even understanding why. For example, they might pursue someone they are attracted to. But, once they get close, they become distant. Then they may repeat this cycle and have no idea why they are doing it. The disorganised-avoidant attachment style is often because of trauma that includes physical abuse, chaotic or scary environments, and/or inconsistent care. It explains why they want closeness, yet have difficulty forming intimate relationships. They fear getting hurt, both emotionally and physically. Or, that the care and love they receive may be taken away.

Trauma bonding, co-dependent relationships, and the push-pull dynamic

Anxious attachment, often rooted in inconsistent childhood care, fuels co-dependency through a desperate need for validation and fear of abandonment. The person tends to neglect their well-being and prioritizes their partner's needs. Similarly, fearful avoidant (disorganised) attachment, coming out of traumatic care, creates a push-pull dynamic that can manifest as co-dependent patterns. Ask yourself (and look into your heartbreak diary to go over the highlighted points). Were you over-functioning for others while struggling with your own needs and boundaries? Then it's likely you were in a co-dependent dynamic, that stemmed from an insecure attachment style. The co-dependency and push-pull dynamic often makes us repeat old patterns.

Imagine a cycle: someone hurts you (it could be abuse of any kind, verbal, gaslighting or passing off demeaning comments as jokes), then they're kind or loving (they're showing remorse/or love bombing you). What the hell! This pattern creates a powerful, unhealthy attachment. You become emotionally dependent on the abuser, the push and pull dynamic feels almost like an addiction and makes it so hard to break free. A push and pull dynamic between couples only makes the uncertainty more attractive. And the craving for an unavailable person's love and approval becomes a toxic pattern. The emotional highs and lows can create a false sense of intensity and passion, making the cycle feel addictive or as if this relationship is your only source of emotional fulfilment.

You can't get off that roller coaster until you see why you've been stuck on it.

Were there intense highs followed by devastating lows in your relationship with your ex? A roller coaster feeling that felt like your emotions were being manipulated? That's not okay. If you were constantly blaming yourself for everything that went wrong, trying to 'fix' things or make sense of their behaviour, or feeling like you couldn't live without them even though they hurt you – it was the trauma bond talking. Trauma bonds eat away at your self-worth and create a feeling of intense emotional dependence. You start to feel like you need that person to survive. You create excuses for their shitty behaviour and minimize how badly they treated you. These are all signs that your reality may have been distorted.

When I think of any of us, stuck in a trauma bond or a toxic push-pull cycle, I'm reminded of a song. 'Windmills of your mind'. 'Round like a circle in a spiral, like a wheel within a wheel. Never ending or beginning on an ever-spinning reel'.

Visualise this. A really tall giant wheel that goes high, really high, it feels like you could almost touch the moon. The whole city is a sharp, long drop away. You are in a seat on that exhilarating but scary ride. You want to get off because you can't take the stomach churn of the downward loop of the ride but you're stuck. Because the giant wheel never seems to stop long enough for you to get off. The unpredictable push-pull dynamic, with its moments of intense connection followed by withdrawal, creates a cycle that feels difficult to break. Just when you think you've mustered the strength to break away, the person throws you some crumbs of affection. Again, you are reeled in. You are back in the cycle of emotional dependency.

When your insecure attachment style is different from your ex's.

Let's suppose that you are an anxious-attached person and you gave your heart to an avoidant-attached person. You craved reassurance from them. They craved closeness but also feared it. It was incredibly confusing for you. One minute you felt deeply connected with them. The next moment they had become distant. How stupid that made you feel – imagining you've found 'the one'. Someone who was so incredibly charming and attentive at the start. But then, the dynamic shifted. They became less responsive, and an emotional wall went up. Just when you started to question everything, they sometimes returned to their former self, only to repeat the pattern.

This push-pull behaviour is typical of a fearful-avoidant attachment style. It can feel like a weaponization of your vulnerability, one day feeling understood, another day bewildered. Their fear of intimacy makes them pull you in and then push you away as things start to feel 'too real'.

You were not imagining things; this is part of the avoidant attached person's pattern.

If you think you'll fix their issues by constantly

reaching out when they are pulling away, trying to seek reassurance (it feels like pressure to them), and over-explaining your feelings (that feels overwhelming) – it won't. It's crucial to understand that this isn't about you being 'too much'. It's about their limited capacity for genuine emotional intimacy at this point in their journey. It is not a reflection of your worth; it's a manifestation of their own unresolved trauma wounds and fear of being hurt again. Understanding an avoidant is fine; it's also helpful in understanding the break-up. But don't wait indefinitely for someone to change. *They need to be willing to do the necessary work*, otherwise the pattern is likely to continue.

How do you heal? By showing up for 'Baby-You', who is hurting in all this.

Your grief may feel raw and fresh, especially the sense of rejection that's triggered by the recent failed relationship. But I hope you can see now that it's got a lot to do with the continued sadness from very old emotional wounds that were caused by the childhood traumas you faced and trying to find your own way to cope with them. Deep down, your heart recognises that the pain is familiar. It's a wound caused by a parent or caregiver. And then by a partner. Someone who should have made you feel safe, but didn't.

I know it feels unbearable to keep chasing love that keeps slipping away. This current, overwhelming grief is not just over the loss of a person or a relationship.

You grieve the childhood where you felt invisible. You grieve the safety you deserved but never had. You grieve the love that wasn't given to you as a child. You have to begin by letting Baby-You feel what they were never allowed to. Thoughts like 'Why? Why does this always happen to me?' are bound to come, it's normal. Let them come and go. But that attachment wound you've been running from doesn't need more avoidance, it needs your attention.

You have tried so many other things to heal. Running from reality, keeping yourself over-busy etc. Try stopping for just a while to let yourself grieve, my dear friend. Give yourself a little daily quiet time. Do it with your phone and devices in flight mode. Time it, if you wish, so it doesn't feel like a lot but you know it is what you made a commitment to do – for yourself. When you sit with your grief, something shifts. The wound starts to close, not because someone else healed it for you, but because *you finally acknowledged it.* You gave it space. You gave it love. You gave yourself what no one else could.

The love you're chasing begins with the love you give yourself. Cliché? Yes. Truth? Oh yes!

EXIT THE HEARTBREAK
EXplain

A letter to your former self

What: Write a compassionate letter to yourself *from before* the relationship. Acknowledge the pain you're experiencing, but remind yourself of your strength and resilience.
Why: Your inner child needs to hear the words of comfort you are craving.
How:

- Start with 'Dear Baby [Your Name]'
- I know you're hurting right now...
- I know you've been hurting for a long time. Right from back when you were the beautiful, precious Baby [Your Name]. All those times when you felt alone in the world. Like when… (Add your specific life incidents, any remarks from close caregivers that made you feel unloved and like you were not of any consequence, or the times you tried to be heard but were not)
- Come to the present moment. My dearest Baby [Your Name], I know that once again, you are feeling hurt and alone. I know that it was horrible the way… (acknowledge the most specific pain points of the break-up)
- Make this very firm promise to yourself. Write it: I promise you Baby [Your Name], *what is past is*

past. I will never let Baby [Your Name] down again. I know it may be tough at times, but I will not betray you, my darling Baby [Your Name] with unthought-out actions again.

- Remind yourself of your positive qualities and past successes. Think of the positive qualities that matter. You know you have them – kindness, helping someone even when you're hurting, etc. Remind yourself in the letter that you are all these things. '*Baby [Your Name], never forget, you are the sherdil, the lionhearted one, with jigra, who didn't get defeated by* (add at least one strength story from your life, one story of success, in this letter to yourself. It could be a memory of standing up to a bully. Or a time you were able to pull yourself together and do something even when you and others just didn't think you could).

Bhaad mei jaye baaki sab kuch. (To hell with everything else.) You have promised Baby-You that you will heal. You will not let Baby-You down again. That is non-negotiable.

Flights of fancy: Tarika's story

I was thirty-one when Nayan, my husband, died. He was thirty-four. He worked with a research company in Dubai. When he was diagnosed with advanced COPD, it was already too late. He died within three months. My only child, my son, was four at the time.

In college, I had fallen in love with Jude. He was attentive, romantic, made a big deal out of special days (red roses on Valentine's Day, gifts on my birthday, even to this day), perfect in every way – except he was from a different religion. With him, I felt beautiful. I hoped to convince my parents to agree to us marrying. But the idea was just not entertained. My mother's face had set in a frown; my father did not speak to me at all. That was the worst. When my mother said I can't marry Jude, my heart sank. Going against their wishes could never be an option for me.

Nayan's match came soon after that. My parents urged me to accept it. He was well-educated, and settled in Dubai. I left my new job as a copywriter. Everyone said I could start again there. That didn't happen though. I got pregnant and had our son in the first year itself. I really can't complain about Nayan and my marriage. It was ok. I would not compare Nayan with Jude but I missed the romance. Sex may have happened when Nayan was sober but never romance. That was for after a few drinks. Then he'd sing songs especially with the word *nayan* (eyes) in them. He loved my eyes. I loved it when he serenaded me.

Rupin was a close friend of Nayan's. He loved him madly. Rupin and I had a warm bond too. We'd cook lots of non-veg stuff when Aman came over. Nayan and Rupin were from the same school. Nayan went into corporate, Rupin went into academia. Within a few years Rupin got married and moved to Ireland. I heard his marriage wasn't going well. We lost touch.

When Nayan died, it was a time of major grief for me. I had no way of supporting my son and me in Dubai. I came to live with my in-laws in Surat. They were a large business family. Life revolved around meals, weddings and shopping trips. I lived with them for six months. It was a loving but completely different set-up from my parents' home. I started feeling the burden of being the widow of their youngest, most brilliant son. Panic would hit me anytime, wondering if this was going to be my life till I die. I became lacklustre even in calls with my parents.

Luckily, my mother asked my in-laws to allow me to live with them in Jaipur. I started working again, writing for a small content company, and I had my parents' support in bringing up my son.

It took me twenty years after Nayan's death to even consider meeting other guys. That was when I met Rajesh Raju on Tinder. He was moody, divorced, but seemed serious about a relationship. He introduced me to his family, included me in their outings. I got to know his sons and his mother quite well. His mother called me often and I started caring for her like a family member, helping Rajesh arrange ambulances for his mom, and rush to hospital with them. I helped arrange his mom's funeral when she passed away. Can you blame me for thinking that there was more to the relationship? But I was stunned at the funeral. He thanked fifty other people but made no mention of me at all. I am North Indian; I clearly looked different from all of them. I felt weird, like everyone must be wondering who is she. He didn't acknowledge me at all. From blow-hot, blow-cold, he soon went just cold. Just some occasional shitty forwards about causes he supports. Once I even contributed to one of them, but did it matter? No. Not even a nice thank-you text from him. It hurt to realise and accept that all he was looking for was sex from me. How convenient that I took on his family responsibilities too.

I strictly forbade myself from even thinking of him.

In all this turmoil – Rupin was the one person I wanted to reach out to. We had reconnected on Facebook but for eighteen years we hardly exchanged any texts. Eight months after things went sour with Rajesh, Rupin's texts started getting a little flirty. By then, we had connected on WhatsApp also. He started asking, 'Who are you seeing in Jaipur?' and when I'd say, 'No one,' he'd text, 'People there must be blind. They should be queueing up!'

By now the texts were happening regularly. He is very old school; his texts were a clean kind of flirty. Sweet stuff like 'It'll be good to hold you in my arms.' I was willing to give it a try. Rupin had been living in Ireland for many years. He used to come to Ajmer to see his mother. I started saying I want to come to Ireland. I was enjoying the back-and-forth chatting. I would stay up nights for it, despite the time difference. He could only text after his lectures were done. I didn't mind sacrificing my sleep though it was tough with my full-time job. After Rajesh's shitty behaviour, I felt optimistic. I could trust Rupin.

I happened to be in Ajmer while he was there. We met for lunch. Strangely, it was a weirdly neutral meeting. All the innuendos had gone. Of course, I told myself, he is preoccupied about his mother being ill.

The thing about Rupin is he'd been such a good friend during my husband's illness that I felt very connected to him. It's not like he's handsome. I probably projected my husband's personality onto him. Like I did with Rajesh. I realised only later that I used to project Jude on to Rajesh just because I'd discovered he was Jude's cousin. And Jude had been my constant reference point in romance.

I booked my Ireland trip for nine days after giving it a lot of thought. I asked Rupin if that would be enough time. He said, 'Yeah.' He never once said make it longer. He ticked all the right boxes you know, he received me at the airport, took time off, took me to see his friends. But the romance just wasn't there. There was no PDA, except to come to my room at night to have sex with the lights off, he never even tried doing it in another room. Not like Nayan. Nothing could deter him. He was keen on it, anywhere, anytime. Rupin didn't tell me I looked good. I took trouble to dress well, even cooked special things, cleaned his house, but there was no appreciation from him.

I expected cuddling, hand-holding but at no time did he say anything. What used to be there in texts even if off and on, now, in person – there was nothing.

I mentioned once that soon it would be time for me to leave. He was more worried I shouldn't miss my flight. I said, 'What's the worst that can happen?' He said, 'I won't be there.' He was to travel for some conference right after I left. At the airport departures gate, I told Aman 'I will miss you.' He just smiled but didn't say it back. I felt pained being parted from him, with no promise, no idea if we would ever meet again. I genuinely felt sad. I regretted staying with him; wasting time on a dead relationship. I should just have stayed in an Airbnb and explored a new country without building hopes around this man.

I even tried to rationalise it. I wondered, why do men go quiet when they are in a bad zone? It's a man-woman thing. Like in the last months before Nayan died, he had just stopped talking.

Even earlier, it was always me initiating conversations, asking Rupin about his day. Never him. At best, he'd forward something. When I came back, the calls dwindled. It had felt right in so many ways. I couldn't believe how it could turn out so wrong.

Maybe I'm the delusional one. I only meet guys who don't want to acknowledge me as a woman in their life. This just felt like another case where I had been foolish again. When Rupin lost his mom, he didn't even get in touch. I saw it on his Facebook. I felt so small. Then a year later he texted to say 'I miss you.' Another time, he messaged, 'Those were the best days of my life.' It took him a year to realise this?

By then I had given up trying with him. I'm unforgiving like that.

Then came Brij Sikarwar, who I met on Tinder. We were from the same community. It mattered to me, because I knew it would matter to my parents. It felt good to just have somebody ask when I'm finishing work, who'd lure me away for coffee, insist on dropping me home; be my plus one after years of me going alone everywhere. He was so enthu! But what a disaster he turned out to be! I knew in my heart something was off, but I ignored it, enjoying the attention while it lasted. Soon my mother made enquiries and we discovered all that he had been saying was a sham. Not only was he not divorced or a single father as he claimed, he had a regular family in another city! It was the biggest embarrassment of my life. Why would he play along with me, when I had been clear from the beginning that I was looking for marriage?

I really can't understand how I keep misreading men.

My mind takes off, imagining five steps forward. Now Rupin also sends me flowers on Valentine's Day. I don't get why he doing it. I say thank you and send a picture of myself with the flowers. Maybe part of me still wants to give him an opportunity to explain why he changed when I went to Ireland. But other than those flowers that still arrive on Valentine's Day there is nothing else.

The truth is I have never broken up with any of the

men I have seen. I always internalise, feel like crap, and move on.

I feel women look down on women who are single. In our community, I feel they look at me and still think: she is a widow. They won't say it openly. But I feel it is so. At 55, I'm aware that people view me as an older woman. I'm conscious of my responsibilities as a parent. My priorities are different.

My sister-in-law used to say 'Stop living in the clouds. Get down to earth. Settle down.' So I don't look for anything now. At best I hope for companionship. Romance? That flight of fancy never really got off the ground. It is not destined for me.

Jude was the best I had. Then you grow up and realise no man is perfect. Years later, Jude and I got drunk one evening, quite drunk; one thing led to another, but honestly there was none of that earlier magic. It felt just yuck.

One of my schoolmates once introduced me to this guy – Pratham. He has been saying for many years that he is crazy about me. He would keep appearing in Jaipur, saying this, but I'd send him away. I felt cynical. Like, where can this relationship go? Pratham is divorced, he used to be a test pilot in the Army, now he flies commercially. He's a single parent like me. At this age, marriage is not something most men want to get into and I'm not ok with living together. I know my family. They'd die rather than tell the world their daughter is living with a man.

After Rupin, and after I turned 55 – all my romantic

notions have been grounded. My son is growing up fast; there's a parade of girlfriends in his life. I don't even want Pratham's proposal right now. I'm not sure I'm ready to share space with any guy. Honestly, I've been so shaken by how I could misread those guys that I keep thinking this too will end. I don't want to be in a situation thinking *kab jayega versus kab aayega, kab aayega!* (When will he go versus when will he come, when will he come!) Maybe if I fall in love with him...

Before the pandemic I was still optimistic. Not anymore. Yet loneliness scares me. With Pratham, I don't even try to dress up or anything. I can't even say take me or leave me because I am not saying take me, but I don't want him to leave either.

This guy shows every sign of being serious and wanting a loyal relationship. He invited me to his daughter's reception. I travelled to Kolkata for it. He looked after me well and introduced me to his family. He has pretty much made Jaipur his hub, spent long periods of time with me and my son. In fact, he's given me a lot of space and time to make up my mind.

So maybe there's still hope for me. Maybe, after all my failed flights of fancy, maybe my dream of landing myself a committed partner might actually take off.

Postscript: A year after narrating her story, Tarika updates that Pratham has proposed marriage to her, and she said yes. She now wears his promise ring. They have decided to spend another year getting to know each other before getting together in life.

Controlled chaos: Yash's story

∞

Ayesha and I became Facebook friends while both of us were dating other people. Cut to four years later. We were both going through our first break-ups. For months we talked like friends, became confidantes. The affection grew. She visited Muzaffarpur – where I lived. If I didn't speak to her even for a day, I would miss her. I told her we should try getting together and 'see where it goes.' She had baggage from her past relationship. He was a narcissist and used to suppress her a lot. My first girlfriend was a narcissist too who made me feel like all my decisions were wrong.

It became Ayesha's goal to not take any shit, including anything that involved us. I also found myself repeating my old patterns of accepting crap. We talked this through; things got a little better. Her ex used to break her confidence about not clearing her CAT entrance. I felt that since I'm in a better place professionally, I can guide her. She had no clarity about what direction she wanted to go in. I used to be stern with her about it. I feel we spend at least 60 per cent of our lives on our professional life. There was pushback from her, not wanting to repeat her old patterns. Physically, it was a bit of a rough patch initially. I felt a lot of performance pressure. She hadn't experienced this before, but she was supportive. There were instances when I couldn't do well. I even saw a doctor, but we agreed it was nobody's fault. Our professional conflicts increased. I felt she was being escapist. She comes from a more well-to-do background than me and we are from different castes. It didn't matter to me. I wanted her to try different things to figure out what she wants. Suppose she said she wants to try cooking, I would have given her data points on it. But she wasn't trying. She was already hardwired.

A year in, I felt we were still where we were at the start. I was trying. I cracked CAT but wasn't happy with my percentile, so I started studying for GMAT. I gave her this example. I told her if you want to gain something, you have to give up something. I would try to motivate her for two-two hours. 'Focus on the long-term benefit.' Still, she'd go out partying with friends. It was like a slap on my face. I started chatting with another girl. One ping led to another, I asked her to get on a video call, but she didn't; she was in a relationship. Two days later, Ayesha came over. We went out for dinner, even danced together. When I went to the bathroom, she opened my mobile. She knows my password. She saw these messages and was very upset. She was like 'How can you ask a girl for a video call?' I thought she was pranking me. I felt I did nothing wrong. That's why I didn't even hide my phone.

One thing about me – I never force anyone. Be it my bro, my mother, I'll give a one-hour monologue, but I give them their space. This incident created trust issues between Ayesha and me. Though we agreed to put it behind us, her suspicions increased. My friends advised me to be patient. Parallelly, I got a good score on my GMAT. Ayesha was in Patna. She used to get

WFH and come to stay with me in Muzaffarpur. Our relationship was still secret. We planned to reveal it to the families once I got a good job. Ayesha was still stuck professionally. There is a two-year gap between us. My ideology is to do all the 'professional settlement' before marriage. After marriage, a couple will experience new things. Plus, they'll have to handle expectations to have a child.

I got into one of the IIMs when the pandemic started. MBA is intense. Meeting so many people was new to me. I started neglecting her. If I had calls with any girls, I saw it as networking, but she wanted full information constantly. I felt like 'Why?' This distrust box has been closed, why keep reopening it? I made sure this 'information asymmetry' is not there. Then our conversations got better. And I got placed.

With Ayesha, I felt I was myself throughout. Our three years together were bliss. I used to listen to her, she was patient with me, we had a blast, danced a lot, we could discuss what we should change. She started taking my advice seriously too. We were both equally confused, equally in sync, the communication was good. Whenever I had frustrations at IIM, she came and met me, so I didn't feel alone. Family don't get study stress. But Ayeshu used to hear out my shouting; she knew 'after the shouting is where my Yash starts.' Just her presence made a difference. At IIM I had started writing comedy. Ayesha would listen to my material.

Once I got placed, I told my father. Dad said 'Let's meet their family.' We are both Biharis but from different castes. Her parents were OK with me. We expected trouble from my mom; she's from a high caste family. Ayesha told me, 'Make sure your mom doesn't make a scene.' How? Mom went out of control. She kept weeping, telling Ayesha's parents, 'Your daughter kept meeting my son secretly. That's not what girls from good families do.' I wasn't off the hook either. 'How could you go against what matters to us as a family?' Winning this battle of who her son marries was proper war for my mom. I called Ayesha to explain that mom reacted badly because her brother had married out of caste, and it hadn't worked out. Ayesha even called my mother the next day to say she'll be the ideal daughter-in-law. It was complete chaos all around.

Pressure intensified from Ayesha's father. My dad jumped in, pushing for more time to plan a wedding. A date was set. Mom's emotional *atyachar* (torture) was relentless. Repeating like a stuck parrot that she had a dream that I may have an accident if I marry Ayesha. I was clear I haven't earned enough; I was being rushed.

I had no way to bring control back into the situation.

By then I was working in Mumbai. Ayesha's parents started making her meet other guys. She goaded me to download dating apps. Her logic? She said, 'I want you but not like this. Your mom's doubt has crept into your eyes.' And then the casual enquiries, 'How's it going on the dating apps?'

One day, I matched on a dating app with a Puja. It started with normal chat. Then this Puja says, 'Can we take it to the next level?' I thought, 'How can I do this and still go back to Ayesha, what does that even make me?' Puja started sexting me. I was shit scared.

Immediately, I messaged Ayesha. 'I have found my answer and it's you, always you; you're the one.' I didn't know Puja was a fake profile created by Ayesha herself. Ayesha was getting both my messages – to her and the ones to the fake Puja. After a bit of sexting, because of my frustration about everything, I texted Puja that 'I can't do it.' All the time I was thinking '*ke bhai, isme kuch rakha nahi hai, niklo.*' (There's nothing in all this, dude, get out.)

Ayesha refused to believe me. She said, 'You were my last ray of hope.' It ended like that, on a phone call. She was already confused between me and her marriage prospects. Now things were looking 'equational not emotional'.

She went on a pilgrimage with her parents; returned and told me she had decided to marry another guy. After the break-up, for months I didn't open my phone gallery; it has more than 10,000 pics and videos of us. I would do anything she said, even dress like a girl, there was never any boundary. We had an Insta profile together, with reels of us dancing, even of our fights. My friend said to me, 'You have to pay your dues to the death of a relationship.'

One day after she got engaged, Ayesha texted me, 'Hey, I had sex with him in the car.'

I acted cool. I said, 'Hope you're having a better time with him than me.'

She says 'I thought it'll help you move on.'

There was no stalking, no messaging from my end.

Recently she forwarded me one of our old posts, 'That was the best part of my life.' It triggered me again. But I can't show her that, can I? In the past, she always came to me for clarity and help. The day she came and said, 'I'm getting married,' what could I do?

She came to me with a decision, not confusion.

Last thing before we parted: I wanted her to at least get a better job. I prepped her for mock interviews, put my heart and soul into helping her get that break. And it happened. It kills me all the time. How I had only wanted the best for her but she couldn't see it. *'Ek baar sun lete yaar meri baat!'* (Just once, you could've listened to me!)

Ayesha got married one month after the break up. I wanted to rip off the band-aid from my emotions. I asked her for the live link to see her wedding. I wanted to be there quietly like a well-wisher. It was painful but it was quick. I saw her participating in everything.

The Google memories keep showing up. I am taking on more work to avoid revisiting our photos. Three days back, again I had a crying session by myself. I reinstalled some dating apps, went on some dates. Nothing is gelling. When women send me emojis or dog reels like Ayesha used to, I feel sick. I haven't tried to reconnect. I respect the sanctity of marriage.

She's there. I'm here. I have to make my peace with that. I will not block her. I want to build a natural insulation within me that we can never happen.

I have realised that with Ayesha, I had been the unconditional me. What we had was the best. I see it only now. I am sorry for everything. About the sexting with Puja too, I thought I'd show it to Ayesha in person. I was going to take complete accountability for my mistake. I wanted to change myself.

I know I have to get through this. I'll take time to heal. I've got a plan going for now.

Operation Damage control:

Action pt. 1: I will join a gym and get fit. Progress: Already happening

Action pt. 2: Go on my first solo trip. Progress: Finally went to Manali on my own.

Action pt. 3: Do an open mic. Progress: Done five sets at IIM as prep. Mostly observational stuff. I'm not ready yet for a bigger stage, but my time will come. Have to work more on spotting the humour; laugh at myself and life.

5

This one's not on you: The narcissistic personality – Know and NO

When I started researching heartbreak with mental health professionals, I was surprised at how often the word narcissist and 'narcissistic personality disorder' (NPD) kept coming up. 'You can't write about heartbreak and not write about NPD and how often it is unrecognised. It is a lot more damaging than people realise,' I was told. I started understanding then that NPD was much more common than many realised and a cause for crushing heartbreaks.

Know what a narcissist is. And why it is seen as toxic.

The term 'narcissist' comes from a Greek myth about an exceptionally beautiful man called Narcissus. He was cruel and self-absorbed, rejecting anyone who sought his love. A nymph called Echo (with a curse to repeat the last words spoken by others) fell in love with Narcissus. She couldn't express her feelings to him because of the curse. Narcissus rejected her and she was devastated. To punish him for his cruelty, the God Nemesis cursed Narcissus to become obsessed with his reflection, unable to eat, sleep or look away from it. He wasted away, yearning for his own image. The story of Narcissus is a cautionary tale about the dangers of excessive self-love, self-obsession and how important empathy is.

It was only when I read about narcissistic personality disorder (NPD) that I recognised the traits of cruelty and lack of empathy in some people whose approval I had been struggling to win all my life. Not everyone has NPD. But it's important you figure out if your ex was a narc. It would explain a lot.

Know the difference. Narcissism and Narcissistic personality disorder (NPD)

It's human to have some narcissistic tendencies, like boasting, looking for admiration or getting high on our own sense of self-importance at times. Social media has only made us crave that validation more. It is when narcissism becomes a pervasive pattern that it is seen as NPD – a mental health condition. Such people feel that they deserve privileges and special treatment. They have a constant need for grandiosity and admiration. Two almost always certain signs of NPD in a person are their shocking lack of empathy and their sense of entitlement.

They will have an unreasonably high sense of self-importance and require constant admiration. A narcissistic person expects to be recognised as superior even without achievements and can go all out to make their talents seem bigger than they are. They are preoccupied with fantasies about success, power, beauty, perfect homes or the perfect partner. Highly narcissistic individuals believe they are superior to others and look down on people they feel are not important. Narcs feel entitled to special favours and will not think twice about taking advantage of others to get what they want. Narcs behave arrogantly, insensitively, brag a lot and lack the ability or willingness to recognise the needs and feelings of others.

Know the narcissistic personality. And tell yourself No. No. No. No. No.

Did your ex have trouble handling any perceived criticism? Narcs have major secret feelings of insecurity, shame, humiliation. They fear being exposed as failures. Yet, they often get aggressively competitive and envious, convinced that others are jealous of them. Their entitlement makes them impatient or angry when they don't receive special treatment. They are hopeless at managing their emotions and behaviour. In fact, people with NPD can't handle stress well and avoid situations where they might fail.

People with NPD have major problems interacting with others and feel easily slighted. A highly narcissistic person will react with contempt and try to belittle others to make themselves appear superior. Gaslighting other people is extremely common behaviour for people with NPD.

I can think of so many people I know who tick those boxes. I wish I could call them out. But, I won't, because I hope to live to tell this tale.

NO more manipulation. NO more guesswork. NO more games

If you've been reading this and nodding away furiously and are convinced that your ex is a narc, then my dear friend, torturing yourself over the breakup is pointless. That ex is forever going to be very hard to change. The best thing the ex has given you is this space or peace or freedom – if you can see it. And if *you* were the one to break-up – mubarak ho (congratulations) on achieving this emotional jailbreak. Even if the ex wants to get back with you, please remind yourself, they had NO empathy for what they put you through. They had NO appreciation of you and what the relationship meant. NO. All they're missing is the validation they fed off you. They still have NO realisation of the problems you tried to discuss with them. It is not in the nature of a person with NPD to give anything to anyone *except what they want to give you.* If by considering giving that narc ex another chance, you think this time you will be in control – NO way! They are still in control. A narc will lie, cheat, twist facts around, confuse the hell out of what actually happened, till it is all a blur to you. And it is not because of you. *It is still always about validation for themselves.*

A fatal attraction: People with trauma bonding patterns and narcissists

A person with a trauma bonding pattern is more likely to get into a relationship with a narc. Their harmful past dynamics, feel familiar and 'safe' with a narc. Narcs often recreate patterns of control and inconsistent affection. And for the poor souls with trauma histories (people like me), who often have low self-esteem, the initial love-bombing and praise from a narcissist gives them intense, addictive validation. Experts also suggest that at a subconscious level, people with past trauma think that, by reliving similar relationship patterns, they'll fix themselves, and believe their love can 'fix' their partner. It becomes a paradox that keeps them in a cycle because their chronic exposure to abusive relationships – and the fear, guilt, low self-esteem (which hadn't gone away anytime) taught them to build a tolerance for unhealthy behaviour. As a result, they are more likely to miss or dismiss red flags that others might run from. Worst of all, when a narc throws out crumbs of appreciation, now and then, it feels incredibly rewarding to the trauma-bonded person, who is used to inconsistency. Sadly, that behaviour only strengthens the bond.

The tragedy of mismatch in two diametrically different people

Trauma victims feel a shame that doesn't belong to them. Narcissists, on the other hand, should be ashamed of their toxic behaviour. But fat chance that they will ever be! Trauma victims take responsibility, even when they shouldn't. Narcissists should take responsibility, but are always unwilling to do it. A trauma victim constantly takes on feelings of guilt and remorse, which don't necessarily belong to them. A narcissist should feel guilt and remorse for their actions but they don't. Trauma victims are often *kuch zyaada hi* (excessively) empathetic. Narcissists lack empathy. Trauma victims feel unsafe because they have been violated in the past. The narcissist violates the other person's safety. Trauma victims are often occupied with managing their own fear and shame. Narcissists, classically, are obsessed only with managing their image and the story that must be spun out for the world.

Trauma victims accommodate people and circumstances much more than they need to. Narcissists should accommodate other people, given what they put the people in their life through. But of course they don't.

You have to say 'Fuck it.' I'm not doing this again.' You have to break the cycle.

Is your ex/partner a narcissist? It is a nightmare cycle to break. But it has to be done.

First thing. Recognise these patterns. That's the only way you'll be able to heal and form healthy relationships. Yeah, yeah, I know you say you're done with all that, but let's just work towards getting rid of this *ex ka bhoot* (shadow of the ex) fully, ok?

Second thing. Stop making excuses for the narcissist. If you think the poor *bechara/bechari* (helpless thing) became a narc because of intergenerational trauma, no, not necessarily. 'Do we assume childhood trauma is a cause for narcissism?' I asked some experts. Their answer was 'absolutely not'. In fact, they said it is lazy to assume that trauma or biology are the only factors in what make a narcissist. Many who became narcs grew up in normal, loving households. So pull back. Recognise that you may have 'Stockholm syndrome'. That's when hostages or abuse victims develop positive feelings towards their captors or abusers. This bond can manifest as sympathy, loyalty, or even affection in the face of danger and mistreatment. Snap out of it!

Third thing. Own up to your part in it. Stop thinking of yourself as helpless.

You went through childhood with the trauma of trying to get a difficult person to be good to you. It's not easy as a child to comprehend that, let alone walk away from it. But in a relationship with a narc, you have the option to say to yourself 'I am done! So totally done. I cannot put myself through this again and again! Not with someone who constantly sets me up for disappointment and pain.' *That 'Fuck it!' has to resound loud and clear in your head.*

And if there are children in the picture, as there were in the story 'Chemical locha' you must, absolutely must remember that *abusing a mother is also child abuse. Not leaving the relationship is not an option.* Staying on in such a relationship will not change the narcissist. It will change and damage you and your children. Witnessing it will emotionally scar your children. You must get out of physical proximity to such a person.

It is our own lack of sense of self and feeling of powerlessness in the situation and relationship that make us hesitate. At this point I must remind you about what I said in chapter 1.

The power that you gave away, you could give it away only because it was yours to give. It is still yours. It cannot go away because it is yours, it belongs to you.

So fuck this stuck-in-a-rut mindset. Fuck the shit that went down in the past. This is now. The wiser you; the 'not a chance in hell, I'm not going through this crap again' you; the never-going-to-lose-myself again for a person, nope, never again' stronger you – must reclaim your precious power. Your power!

That story about you as the victim must be retold. Change your self-talk.

All of us tend to get attached to the idea of being a victim. I'm no exception. We have to take responsibility for what happened. Obsessively talking about your ex or how you were wronged is counterproductive. *Overidentifying as a victim only sabotages your future choices.* Just accept (to yourself) that you were to blame too. For your choices. For picking the wrong person. And for allowing unacceptable behaviour to continue.

Be grateful it is in the past. (If it isn't, I hope you're in therapy with someone excellent and setting priorities and timelines.) I can again only say how sorry I am for what you've been through with that narc ex. But let's look at the single most important thing in this: You are out of that toxic relationship and period in your life. The person you lost wasn't a loving partner but a harmful presence that was depleting you. That narcissist was a manipulator, not a soulmate. Yes, there are bound to be a whole lot of memories – good and not so good. But even at the risk of sounding harsh, I'll have to say this. Because understanding this is vital for you to heal:

The side you saw to your ex as things fell apart, that was their true self. Without the facade.

Their manipulative tactics weren't affection – they were about control. Their dishonesty wasn't a mistake – it was intentional exploitation. You were a means to their end. You didn't lose love; you gained freedom from toxicity.

Narcissists can only mimic love for their own needs.

Please read that again. To heal, accept that you were used, not loved. This escape required great courage. Now, you can find peace and make space for a happier story. You deserve real love and respect, my friend. Don't settle.

Chemical locha: Juhi's story

I have developed a mechanism to just move on. Whatever life throws at me, I get through it and move on.

My dad died when I was three. I moved in with my Nana-Nani. They were both professors at Kanpur university and always in sync with each other. My mother wanted me to get married early. I wanted to wait till I met someone perfect for me, like Nana-Nani. But mom felt that in arranged marriages, love is not some heart-racing realization but comes gradually after sex and after time. I don't know in what order it was supposed to happen. In college I was a tomboy, participating in everything I could. People were shocked I agreed to an arranged marriage. But once I did, I decided to trust the elders' experience and judgement. I didn't want to think anything but optimistic thoughts. The few times that I met Nitin before our marriage, I told myself not to panic. That love would follow.

On my wedding night itself he banged my head against the wall and said, 'You better not think of looking at any one or I'll beat you.' His mum too was violent, and his sister was bipolar. He was in the Army and an alcoholic even before marriage. The alcoholic part, I realised a few days after we got married. I tolerated a lot because I thought that's how it was. He was the first man to touch me, my husband, the father of my kids. On many days I didn't know if I loved him or hated him. Really, it was as if someone had done some locha to my brain. In *Munnabhai MBBS*, they explain love as something that creates some kind of chemical imbalance; the hormones go crazy. I thought, is this why I can't even walk away from him?

What was the problem with me that I couldn't get away, save myself and my children from a man like that. Seriously, what happened to my brain in those years? A large part of me thought I was to blame for triggering him.

I was living like a disjointed person. I loved the fauji life. I would be vivacious outside and quiet in the house. Everyone who knew me could see I had become subdued after marriage. I wouldn't even have chai if it wasn't teatime. Or look directly at anyone in case it flared up the violence. He'd keep saying 'You are so fat; you're not even like a woman. You are like a boy.' Many times, in his fit of anger, like *agar chole ke saath pyaaz nahin kata* (if I forgot to cut onions to go with the chick peas) he would throw us out of the house. I'd keep thinking only in the immediate moment. Like, right now we have to wait till he opens the door. It took a long time before my will to leave him grew stronger. Sometimes, even my mother-in-law would say, 'Why are you with him? You should leave.' He'd come early morning and bend down in front of me and start apologising for what he did last night. I actually couldn't remember what happened. I would prefer to forget and say, 'I forgive you.'

I started living a dazed double life. Away from home, I looked happy; I was temporarily happy. At home, I blocked out hours from the days. I used to think I can't deny my husband his pleasure, even if he was drunk. But it became so much. When he'd come home and bash me, I'd have violent thoughts of killing him. He'd hit me and especially Suraj, our middle child who had autism and a sleeping disorder. It was only diagnosed when Suraj was two and a half. By then I had separated myself physically and emotionally from Nitin – as much as I could. I wanted to get help for Suraj, my baby, once I realised he had special needs. Nitin was in denial about it. I kept trying to get information on where to get the right help.

I had gone with Suraj to Chennai to get early intervention. Around then, Nitin was caught in an affair with an officer's wife and was court martialled. Initially, I believed I needed to support him. I was a fool. In the court martial itself, others backed away from that girl who was known to sleep around. I still tried to believe the best. I used to think, look, no one has seen them together, maybe he's being framed.

My older son who was in Class 6, came and said, 'Ma, why are we staying here?' He had read about this kind of situation. After the affair, I couldn't turn a blind eye to Nitin's behaviour. I couldn't take him anymore. I started to lock my door from inside. Through that haze of forgetting, forgiving, not knowing if he could change as he would promise sometimes, one day, with no plan in mind, I packed my things and left for my mother's house. When you are completely broken, you find strength suddenly from God knows where. When I look back, I think, how did I even survive those years? I filed for divorce on the grounds of domestic violence. It got into a court case.

I had been hanging on by a thread. Nitin's affair and the court martial snapped the thread for me.

Life works strangely. Suddenly we got news Nitin had been hospitalised. We were told he'd got organ failure, liver cirrhosis. He went into coma and died within 24 hours. My older son went into severe depression. He lost twelve kilos. I went from hospital to hospital trying to figure it out. Nitin had wanted to give my children ₹100,000 as a lifetime settlement when I separated from him. I laughed at the ridiculousness of it. 'Okay, *ek laakh rupaye ki mala inko pehna ke khud hi pehen lo.*' (Fine, get a garland made for 1 lakh rupees, put it on the kids, then wear it yourself.) But because he died after we had only one hearing in court, I started getting his pension. Earlier I used to beg him to help with the son's special education. Just a week before his death, he made his mom the nominee. She got all his other assets, the lump sum of ₹5,000,000 on leaving the Army. She kept it all and didn't even give my son his father's TV which he asked for. Now she wants to stay with us; says she wants to give us the money. Hah.

I didn't even want to see the face of another human. I was in full survival mode. When I decided 'enough' and moved out, many people discouraged me, including mom. Reluctantly, she made space for us in her house. With barely any money to manage, I'd make a monthly budget with my kids, we'd even plan, 'This much for ice cream.' But because mom had been a widow for so long, she would keep trying to control every little thing I did. So, I decided I needed to move to Mumbai. Everyone told mom, just see, she'll be back. That's another thing

I'm learning about myself. The moment someone says something negative to me, I take it as a challenge. I was determined to show her that I could do fine on my own. Only Maasi gave me the support I needed and that was enough. My mother started pushing me to start seeing someone again. I realised I had never really experienced love. I always believed there is a soulmate for everyone. I prayed I'd find mine.

That's when this other guy, Rajat, came into my life. He was in marketing, good-looking, confident. This time around, I was totally in love. If we weren't together, we'd be on the phone for a long time. When you're in love, you don't realize how it consumes you.

Maasi felt uncomfortable about him. He moved to Delhi around then and I started to feel things change. I said, 'I thought we had a commitment.' Here I was crazily in love and suddenly he was behaving like I didn't exist. He said 'What? What relationship? We were just getting to know each other.' That's really the time that I had a major heartbreak. When somebody dumps you, you feel so shit, you keep getting through every day with disbelief. Like how can somebody just cut you out. I'd keep pleading with Rajat, at least talk to me. I was a begging idiot. I now look back and want to slap this person I had become.

I would come home from work and keep crying. I just couldn't stop. My kids would counsel me. Maasi found out that he was seeing someone else. It didn't work out apparently. Later he moved to Africa and married some other woman. Imagine! For this shithead, I neglected my kids.

After I realised this and maybe my guilt played a role, my only focus became kids and work; work and kids. I neglected my friends too. My kids started saying, 'Mom you need a life.' I was in depression, but the time I spent on work started showing results professionally.

It takes time to be able to see yourself with distance.

This experience showed me I needed to prioritise my life, my kids and my career. Later I realised it could have been much worse. All that craving for a soulmate, such a waste. It's good I got that out of my system. I don't need it.

Even now, years later, it takes me a lot to open up to somebody. I can't trust people, especially not a man. If, even after I tolerated everything, Nitin could have that affair, and Rajat could turn around and say 'What relationship?' – how do I trust anyone else again? While you're in love, you're blinded. Your friends can see the person is all wrong, but your brain is all fried with that chemical locha. Until four years ago I used to visualise how I'd react if Rajat came in front of me. Would I slap him or thank him for helping me realise what was important for me?

Helping other women gives me purpose. I work in the NGO sector to fight to repeal discriminatory laws, especially against people with disabilities. We work across many states. There are people who say 'Juhi, what're you trying to do, this law cannot be repealed.' But I have managed to have 22 laws repealed. I am part of a major support group for people dealing with violence. Many don't have the courage to make a move. If someone wants to escape; the shelter homes are terrible. People were once telling this newly married woman who was being abused to go to a shelter. I'm a call away from people who need to confide in someone who understands or get legal help. Yesterday this lady who was being beaten and still hesitated to ask the husband to get out, called. She was still thinking ke '*bada anyaye hoga.*' (That'll be a big injustice) Imagine! Just listening to how I could break free with three kids, with no *jaan pehchaan* (connections) and my special needs kid has encouraged many people. In fact, I see that where there's a special needs child, it often ends up breaking up the marriage. My story gives strength to others.

Being destroyed almost, so many times, has shaped me into becoming stronger. I've started imagining myself as unstoppable. Like I'm the phoenix, rising from my ashes. I want to get it tattooed on myself.

6

Love languages, apology languages: What they add up to

What we often remember about a relationship is how the person expressed their love. Some are skilled at saying things that make you feel good. Others have a talent for picking perfect gifts every time. It's also about us, *how we experience and express* love for the other person. These are called love languages. Understanding your love language and theirs, will show you how sometimes it can seem so great but yet, we still read it wrong.

The five love languages:

1. *Words of affirmation:* This love language puts value on expressing affection with praise, encouragement and words of love ('I love you,' 'You're so talented,' 'I love how you...'), and hearing positive affirmations about themselves and the relationship.
2. *Quality time:* This centres around giving someone your undivided attention. It means being present and focused when you're together, having meaningful conversations and doing things together without distractions like phones or other people.
3. *Acts of service:* For these people, actions speak louder than words. They feel loved when their partner does helpful things like run errands, share the load with

chores or ease your responsibilities. The thoughtfulness and effort behind the act are what resonate.

4. *Receiving gifts:* This love language is about tangible symbols of love. It's not necessarily about the monetary value of a gift but what the person put of themselves into it. Meaningful gifts or surprises show that the person was thinking of them.
5. *Physical touch:* These people feel loved through physical affection like holding hands, kissing, cuddling, hugs with more contact or shoulder or back rubs. Basically for these people, touch gives a sense of connection and security.

How to read your emotional pain through the lens of love languages

Our expectations of our partners are usually based on the love language we most crave. We should also be sensitive to what love language matters to them. If two people have entirely different love languages, there will be a mismatch, and this can impact the relationship.

If what you need is different from what you get, you need both good observation and good communication. Think about what you and your ex's love languages were. Were you both communicating with each other about what mattered to you? Was that need being met?

1. *Observe how they expressed love:* How did your ex usually show love to others? People often give love in the way they prefer to receive it. For example, someone who frequently offers help might have 'acts of service' as their primary love language.

2. *Play back their complaints:* What did they often complain about in their relationships? Not just yours. Their unmet needs can point to their love language. Someone who felt ignored in childhood or past relationships might put value on 'quality time' from you.
3. *Notice what they asked for most often:* If someone constantly asked their loved ones for help with tasks, 'acts of service' could be important to them. Or, if they often wanted to spend more one-on-one time, 'quality time' might be their love language.
4. *Reflect on what made them feel most loved:* Think about times they seemed particularly happy. What was happening? Was it a thoughtful gift, a heartfelt compliment, dedicated time spent together, a helpful action or physical affection?

   I must emphasise that the idea is NOT to have you reopening the door that is closed but to be more balanced in your relationship audit. How do you feel after reading this? Was it all on them, or are there bits that you could have played differently?
5. *Going forward:* The most straightforward way to learn someone's love language is to ask them. Have an honest conversation in a relaxed mood about what makes them feel valued. Notice how they respond to different expressions of love. Do they light up when you offer a compliment or seem more touched when you help with a chore? Their reactions can give you valuable cues. Consider their history: past relationships will influence someone's love language and listening, really listening from your heart, will

tell you what they value. For example, in the story, 'No coincidences', it would seem that Andy's love language is 'physical touch'. The sexless years with Jill, the love of his life, made 'physical touch' a validation of love in every relationship that came after. So, if a woman involved with him isn't into 'physical touch' as a love language, there can be trouble ahead.

Why 1+1 need not equal 2. The limitations of love languages.

While love languages are definitely useful in understanding how a person expresses love, they don't always give a complete picture of love, true emotion or predict a break-up.

Doing something superficially vs. out of genuine emotion: Someone might perform acts of service or give gifts because they know it's their partner's love language, but it doesn't automatically mean they fully get you or are committed to you. The *intention* and *emotion* behind the action are crucial and might be missing even when the right love language is being spoken. For example, in the story, 'Mentor tormentor', we see how Manpreet is swept off his feet by his lover Baljot's astute understanding of gift giving, especially to a village boy with no exposure to fancy living. Manpreet tells us, 'If I told him any of my interests, he would indulge me. Like, I like cricket, he didn't, but he would book tickets so I could see it. Or on my birthday, he gifted me the latest Apple phone.'

There's also another way of interpreting this. Some

might call it love bombing, with an intent to manipulate.

Manipulation: Some people can tap into their partner's love language and use it to play on their needs, without genuinely caring for their well-being. For example, someone might shower 'words of affirmation' on their partner to keep them in the relationship, without long-term intent. In the story, 'Sapota sadness', Esha recounts, 'I remember waking up and he'd be staring at me and I'd say "What?" and he'd say, "You are very beautiful." Or if I wore something, he'd say, "Wowww" with his eyes lit up. Then out of the blue one day he comes and says, "My parents found someone for me."'

Effort doesn't equal love: Consistently speaking someone's love language requires effort, but effort alone isn't a guarantee of love. A person might diligently meet their partner's love language needs only out of obligation. Like, for us in India and in many cultures, it is expected that a partner will be beside us, supporting us during a family bereavement. They could be physically present but all the while be busy texting a new love interest. What does that love language count for, then?

Broader emotional needs: Someone might feel 'loved' according to their love language but still feel disconnected in other crucial emotional areas. Beyond being compatible in love languages, love needs so much more. Emotional security, trust, respect, shared values, a match of intellectual wavelengths – I could go on and on.

Love languages: Might feel blissful and yet not predict a break-up

Someone I know had a boyfriend who would constantly, repeatedly and in different ways keep telling her he 'adored her', how much he desired her, how his family would be blown away by her, how she would love his town, how he loved her eyes, how he felt her eyes looked right into his soul, how just listening to her voice could get him hard etc. He constantly gave her all the words of affirmation she craved. Her ex had been a complex, insecure man who often brought her down as a woman. And along came this new man in her life, healing those wounds, filling that void and it was all good – until the day she found herself asking him what he really felt about her. Did he see a future together? The next thing she knew, he had started distancing himself from her. His texts became extremely irregular – just impersonal updates about his life without any mention of the previous refrain of 'I adore you'.

The woman was a mess. We spoke a lot, did a relationship audit and concluded that while his 'words of affirmation' may have been authentic as love languages went, but the crux of it was in their attachment styles. She was an anxious attached style person and he was a fearful avoidant. At the first sign of her getting too close, he panicked and wanted an 'out'.

Love languages, apology languages, breakup languages: Read them all

I should add – only a difference in love languages doesn't

automatically mean two people are incompatible. Just as with love languages, people have distinct apology languages. Meaning: What makes an apology feel sincere and complete to you. There are five apology languages: Expressing *regret*, accepting *responsibility*, making *amends*, genuinely *repenting* and requesting *forgiveness*.

What you need as *the only acceptable apology* may be different from the way your ex apologised (if they did). This is pretty crucial, because an apology, delivered in a different apology language from yours may feel insincere to you. Similarly, people also have break-up languages. How one person prefers to end things is their breakup language. It may not be your preferred break-up language but then break-ups are rarely caused by just one factor. Communication breakdown, lack of trust, different life goals, infidelity, emotional immaturity can all add up and lead to a break-up.

Differences and conflicts are bound to come up. That's why it's important to understand these things better, to pull yourself out of the 'but we were so good together, why didn't it last' mindset. At least, let's learn to communicate our needs. How we like to be shown we are loved or made up with. And you know now, sex is just one part of it.

Mentor tormentor: Manpreet's story

My nature is very different. I feel I am not normal. Normal people, they want to get married. I used to shy away from it. Nature, boys, girls, all animals, I felt love for everything.

Eight years ago, I'd gone to a farmer's fair in Hisar to buy seeds. I was twenty-seven then. I noticed a man of around fifty at the next stall, looking at me. He introduced himself as Baljot. When I said I was a farmer, he started telling others that his sons went abroad, but 'Look at this boy Manpreet, he's smart, sticking to agriculture. That's the future.' He took my phone number. I thought he was just missing his sons.

Next day Baljotji called saying 'I liked talking to you.' He started calling me daily, normal conversation like what's my work routine, my favourite food, my favourite colour, many things I'd never thought about. He remembered every detail like how I like karele but only bharwaan. He shortened my name. '*Kaisa hai mera Preet?*' He usually called me after a few drinks every evening. I looked forward to his call. His voice always low, so personal, so warm, jaise he had also waited the full day, as I had, for our call. Some time back I had lost my father. I started feeling good. After months of talking like this daily, for two-two hours, he said 'let's meet'.

I didn't know what my sexual identity was at that time. A guy once tried to get close to me. I didn't like it.

But when Baljot said, 'Let's make a plan to meet, Preet,' it felt right. We'd grown close already on the phone. We had a lot in common, like love for nature. I said, '*Ji, milte hain.*' He planned for us to meet in Rohtak. I took a bus from my village; he received me in a big car. We went to a five-star hotel. He was like an angel, so caring. His eyes were moist when he hugged me. I felt maybe he was consumed by loneliness.

In the room, we had tea. He said, 'Let's have a drink,' but I said no. My father died early because he drank heavily. He insisted, 'Have a beer at least.' He then said, 'I still remember every word from that night. There is so much purity in you, you take a place for me as God, don't ask why, I think of you first; God comes second.'

I was surprised but I liked it. I wondered what was so special about me. He described my clothes from our first meeting, which I didn't remember myself. He kept saying, 'You are unique, my Preet, there is something magnetic about you.' By then we were both high. He gave me a night suit he had got for me. We lay down together. He hugged me. It felt good. I hadn't thought about what was going to happen; really, I hadn't. When he started kissing me, I started liking it. I felt as if from two we had become one, that we'd be part of each other. I didn't mind what he did at all. I felt like we had reached paradise.

We started meeting every alternate month, getting closer each time. When we parted, we had tears. I used to feel like what's this punishment, to be separated. I learned that he lived with his wife; his kids were in Canada. He and his wife also had Canada Permanent

Resident cards. His wife spent more time in Canada with their children. Baljot and I travelled to so many places – Udaipur, Jaipur, Sikkim, Goa, Kashmir. With him, I liked everything – fields, rain, cold. If I told him about any of my interests, he indulged me. For example, I like cricket, which he didn't, but he'd book tickets for me. For my birthday, he gifted me the latest Apple phone. I could never give him anything expensive in return, so I refused to take it. He stopped talking to me for a month. 'Why are you not taking it? It's not like I'm trying to buy you.' That was our first misunderstanding. Like this, six years passed. He said we'd get a place in Calcutta; that my family responsibilities were his. He just wanted me close. He even met my family, as my friend, but our relationship was kept secret from his family. He had my passport made and said he wanted to take me to Switzerland.

Once, in Ambala, we were to go for a movie. I'd started to drink a little with him. We had some drinks and reached the mall when Baljot said, 'I'll introduce you to a person who'll look after you even more than me.' I was shocked, thinking, 'Is he joking?' He hugged me and started crying loudly. I asked him, 'How can you suggest such a thing?' The mall was packed. 'You think anyone can take your place?' I kept insisting, 'What's happened? Tell me.'

He said he had blood cancer. I felt as if I lost the world in an instant. Why did God do this to me? He said, 'I wish I could die in your arms, but I have to spend these last months with my family.' I felt as if my heart had burst. My brother and bhabhi, even Baljot used to say, 'Get married, Manpreet.' I used to think, 'No. I can't divide my love for you with anyone.' After he told me about the cancer, I was so upset I sat down outside a shop. He said one report was due, but the doctors were clear. It was a matter of months, maybe weeks. We cried and separated.

One full month passed. I kept praying for a miracle. I tried calling Baljot many times. I didn't have his address. I tracked him through a sarpanch connection, saying I met him at Darbar Sahib in Amritsar, and that it was something urgent. Nothing more. So, this sarpanch went personally to Baljot and said Manpreet is looking for you. The sarpanch made him dial my number. Baljot was livid. 'Why did you take it to the sarpanch?' I said, 'Are you crazy? I'm not going to tell anyone our love story. You are in my blood. You tell me you have blood cancer, didn't you think what's going to happen to me?' He cut the call. I even went to see a doctor in a mental hospital. I couldn't tell anyone I had been with him. I told the world I was depressed because a girl dumped me and married someone else. I kept trying to call Baljot, he kept cutting my calls.

Then he abruptly took one call and told me he didn't have blood cancer; it was a severe case of kidney stones. For the first time, I wondered if anything he said was true. I asked Jaswinder, a Facebook contact, to introduce me to other older men, to find out more. Can you believe it? Jaswinder sent me Baljot's photos. How cruel can life be? I told Jaswinder there must be a mistake; this man was very sick. But Jaswinder was certain; he'd met Baljot just two days ago. I dug deeper, found out Baljot had been telling people I spoiled his life. One man asked me, 'Why are you obsessed with him? Let him go.' This was two years ago. I lost faith in God. I was so angry, I felt my face should be imprinted on Baljot's.

I tried to replace him in my heart. Jaswinder introduced me to some guys. They had other demands that didn't work for me. The question of 'why?' wouldn't go away. Why would he lie about cancer to me? His false tears. Why couldn't he be honest? Say he wanted to move on? We put a *patti* (blindfold) on our eyes in love. We blind ourselves. Love is a useless thing. It became the torment of my life. I felt that if I hadn't met Baljot, I could have lived a normal life. I even tried having sex with a woman; it was not for me. After him, I try. I want to feel a person is there for me. I want to get to know them. But for most people, the focus is only on sex. In seven years, I feel like I've lived a whole life. I've lived through hell. I wasn't able to give his place to anyone else, while he kept living a normal life, getting boys. I kept yearning for just fifteen minutes with him. My mind was so clouded that I never asked myself – what would I do with those fifteen minutes? I only wanted that little time, to see him, to get that craving out of my soul.

I asked a guy to secretly arrange a meeting. He told me he'll get another guy into the act to attract Baljot there. Baljot came, expecting a threesome. It was a foggy night. He was sitting outside on a charpai, warming his hands over a small bonfire. He was shocked to see me, but started talking to me in his soft voice, 'How are you, dear Preet? How are things at home?' I went numb.

Everything that had been running through my mind since he lied to me, all went blank. He was pouring stiff pegs. I wasn't used to drinking anymore. I had been so miserable in my yearning that I only kept looking at him. We even had sex that night. The other guy went off to another room. I was so sick in my head and drunk, I started throwing up. Baljot was so clever; he got me emotional, then high, and then he left. At no point did he tell me why he removed me from his life so abruptly.

I'm a sarpanch now. I solve others' problems but I can't talk to anyone about mine.

I tell myself I'm over him. In my time alone, I know I am not. I feel angry with myself most of all. How did I become so weak? All I can make out is that he had enough of me. For him, it was pleasure. For me, it was love.

Sapota sadness: Esha's story

∞

I grew up in Warangal in a typical Telugu family. I was put into IIT coaching from Class 8 – to give you an idea of how seriously they took academic achievement. My mum was clear, 'If you're in a relationship, you're not doing well. That's for people who have no option in life.' And 'If you don't study, we'll get you married to some idiot.'

In my fourth year at IIT Kanpur, it hit me that I had missed out on this whole dating thing because of my parents' rules. Amrit had been my classmate for four years; we even worked in an NGO together. Around when I had got placed, he started giving me attention. My friend Manavi said, 'Amrit really likes you.' It encouraged me to ping him. I started opening up with him, including about my recently being diagnosed with depression. He was the kindest person I had ever met. He told me his mom passed away when he was a kid, that he recently broke up with his girlfriend, that I was one of the few who knows this. I was curious – how was he so in control even after all that?

The final-year college prom was coming up. I thought he'd ask me. We all were off on a road trip. He sat next to me in the car; we cuddled etc. Then later he went and sat in another car. I couldn't understand it. When the prom registration came up, Amrit didn't ask me. I only asked him. 'No, I'm going with someone else,' he said. That he wanted to give it another try with his ex, a senior, who was back on campus.

I felt rejected and unattractive. How was this even possible? He hadn't mentioned anything about her in all our chats. I had already planned that this year I'd go to prom, celebrate V-Day with him. I had thought, with him I wouldn't feel empty any more. Women around me were dating multiple guys. Girls are not supposed to get rejected. The shame kept washing over me in waves. I thought I'll convert that 'no' into a 'yes'.

I felt so bitter and there was Amrit, kind, even the way he let me down, always checking on me. I had to keep seeing him at the NGO we were placed at. I still thought I could win him back. I asked, 'Is it because I don't look good?' I've been getting teased and bullied about my dark skin forever. I used to feel ashamed, thinking if I apply haldi daily, I'll be fair, I'll be beautiful. Your parents' issues get dumped on you. I wasn't permitted to wear anything except Indian clothes and the dupatta always. But in school on Saturdays, you could wear jeans and T-shirt. My mom made sure that I wore dupattas even with that.

'When someone is talking to you, they need to look at your face, not your body,' she would say.

The internal shame is validated when you're rejected externally. If I got a compliment, I used to always feel they were being fake.

I was devastated by the prom rejection. I came back crying uncontrollably to the hostel and missed Manasi's birthday. She stopped talking to me. Those were two brutally lonely months. I was 20. Until then life had only been engineering books, which weren't going to help me from feeling lousier about myself.

I would replay that car scene and feel the joke was on me. That he was using me to make his ex jealous. You feel stupid that you were blind. All you do is add another layer of hurt to yourself. I decided to observe my phases. Extra energy, anger, depression, when I couldn't get out of bed, or get triggered by every little thing. Or get argumentative; keep debating unnecessarily with the professor. Or be a jerk; see Amrit with this woman and say, 'Why are you following me?' The emptiness made me do crazy, impulsive things.

Cut to guy number two, Mukesh. We sat next to each other in office. Basically, handsome, tall, gora, Delhi guy. I was instantly attracted to him but thought this time I won't ping. I won't give a fuck – whatever happens, happens. Very fast we had gotten into seven-hour-long phone calls. I knew everything about him. I didn't open up so much this time. Still, I don't know when the relationship changed into Mukesh saying things like, 'Look, you can't change the fact that you're dark. At least go to the gym. Lose weight and try to look hot.' I thought he was interested in me but these were not statements of somebody who is into you. One particular time, I had gone to Warangal; he hooked up with someone on Tinder. When I brought up the fact that I didn't like this, he turned it on me saying, 'Sapota, if you go on a Tinder date, the guy will just walk away.'

A narcissist will turn everything on you. If I said 'I have a nice name, Esha – use it. I don't like you calling me Sapota,' Mukesh would say 'Now you're offended about that? You can't even take a joke?' Or if I found the confidence to say I didn't like something, he would again act totally surprised and say, 'Huh? When did I say that?' I used to think am I imagining it.

Just to show Mukesh I am attractive, I went on dating apps and started making out with guys. And Mukesh would say, 'Arre yaar, guys in their 20s are always horny. Ladke toh desperate hote hain. No one will want to actually be with you.' I used to have an old song playing in my head, '*Jaoon kahan bata aye dil.*' (My heart, tell me, where do I go?)

It was confusing because Mukesh would call me daily, for hours. I never told him I had a crush on him. I was scared after Amrit. I had zero intuition about whether a guy even liked me. Mukesh would talk about another girl; how hot she was. The blind optimist in me would think his interest in that girl will fizzle out; after all it's me he talks to. The irony is that I never opened my heart to him, he just kept breaking mine.

Even his name for me – Sapota. It hit the rawest nerve of my insecurity.

I've always felt that learning anything new is difficult but once you keep at it, it isn't so tough. I looked at relationships as something I still had to learn. You get into one hoping to find comfort, even when it gets toxic. How stupid is that? The logical answer is self-love but that's easier said than done. So, instead, I started reading up more about narcissistic personalities. Around then Mukesh's office changed; he moved away from me. I started feeling some amount of peace. I joined a pottery class, made some friends. I thought I'd get there; that my life would be better once I was in a better relationship.

I realised that something in me had always made me prone to being around narcissists. But at least it got me talking to a therapist.

The next two years I decided to date with a vengeance. I was on dating apps quite a lot. I'd still be too innocent because on a date the guys would initially be super nice, then sooner or later they would come up with the 'Let's keep it casual' thing. I used to wonder what about me screams casual to them. The same story kept unfolding. Some would lead me to believe they were invested; it would get into a physical thing too. But again, they'd say they weren't interested in a relationship. Round and round it went, till it reached a point where I didn't want to date any more.

I decided to set myself two small ten-year goals. Just to have one guy and one friend for whom I was enough. Every time it fell apart, I'd blame myself. There was a lot of shame in who I was, my looks, and my mood swings. I did therapy. It got me to see that if I had set any other goal like trying for IAS, would I give it 10 years? Or would I have said 'OK it's not happening; why keep giving more energy to these two goals?' My core belief till then was that a good social network is essential. I need human relationships if I want to stay healthy until my old age. My therapist helped me to listen to my body physically. I started seeing how anxiety was also affecting my body. I tell you even the mental health goals were giving me anxiety and I decided to give that up too as a goal.

Without friends, I wasn't getting my emotional need for connection from real life. Reading books, getting into other people's stories, satisfied that to an extent. I started cooking, travelling, made my first overseas trip and my first solo trip – things I never thought I'd do on my own. But that aching loneliness, what does one do? Loneliness, they say, is like smoking thirty cigarettes a day. I would wonder if I switched off my WhatsApp for three weeks, would anyone even think of me?

I turned twenty-nine and my parents' pressure to get married became unbearable. In South Indian families especially, thirty is too late for a girl to get married. It reached a point where my mom stopped talking to me for four months. I finally agreed to speak to guys from matrimony apps. You meet some pretty weird, conservative people there. They don't want a very educated girl or one who's earning too much. It started to feel nauseating. I gave it a break. Again, mom stopped talking to me. The stress gets too much. That period of up and down with characters from dating apps was exhausting too. I met a guy called Shubham. He wasn't into casual, so we ended up dating for a year. Finally, it fizzled out because I felt he was cheating and if I'm honest, I was bored of him. He was my first real boyfriend. In retrospect, it did teach me that online relationships are bullshit.

I met Prabhakar during my MBA. I noticed how he helped others without being asked; his relationship skills were top-notch. He was the love of my life. The one that hit me hardest. We dated for a year and a half, then on-off for another year. Prabhakar was handicapped. One of his legs didn't work after a spinal cord surgery;

some nerves were damaged. He used the other leg to drag himself along. He used a wheelchair. We didn't let it get in the way of our relationship. Physically too, we worked around it. Even the fact that he used urine bags at night. He could have used his disability to get admission anywhere but he didn't – not even on a diversity card. Even in college, he'd treat it like it was just fine. Then his parents started to push him to do intensive physiotherapy and work with a startup.

My biggest issue was he wasn't giving me time. We began arguing a lot. All through MBA, I took care of him but he didn't want to get married to me. He started saying things like 'you are like my wife' but also that as he got older, his health would get worse. Even his parents would need looking after. It would all land on the person he married. He was categorical that he wanted to live independently and marriage was off the cards.

With Prabhakar, my heart just expanded. I used to find joy in caring for him. I felt needed. He'd give me a lot of attention. If I had to rate him on any of the love languages, he was intermediate to expert level. In college he had a studio apartment and I was always there. I'd mostly sleep there; we were essentially living together. I remember waking up and he'd be staring at me and I'd say 'What?' and he'd say, 'You are very beautiful.' Or if I wore something, he'd say 'Wowww' with his eyes lit up. Or if I came back from somewhere he'd hug me hard.

Then out of the blue one day he comes and says, 'My parents found someone for me. She is very keen to get married. And you know I'm dependent on my parents.'

Later I learned that the woman was an orphan, and it's not like she was dumb. She worked at an MNC. I couldn't figure out what her scene was. How did she agree to be his caretaker? In a normal arranged marriage market, it is very unusual. He kept insisting, 'Esha, you are the real love of my life,' and 'Look, I hate marriage but I depend on my parents to care for me. I have to agree to this.'

What was really fucked up was telling me he didn't want to marry her. Till fifteen days before the marriage, we were texting intensely. We even met at a hotel before he was to go off for the wedding. He said he wasn't even buying any wedding clothes. That he'd insisted on no wedding function, just a simple village temple wedding, that he wasn't inviting anyone from our MBA course. Next morning my friends sent me a link where it said very clearly that Prabhakar was engaged to this girl. So, imagine when he is sleeping with me in a hotel, he's already engaged to this girl. I showed it to him and he panicked. He still continued saying, 'You're more important to me.' I believed everything. I saw that the Facebook announcement was made by his fiancée. It still gave me hope that he wasn't invested in her.

The real heartbreak for me was to see his new WhatsApp DP after marriage. I was very confused. After saying he was not interested in this girl, he puts up that DP of him and his wife in wedding clothes. It convinced me: he's married; he's moved on. And for me that is not right – to engage with a married man.

It was the worst six months of my life. I kept going over all our photos. Even when I slept, I dreamt of him. The longest streak I had was to go three days without crying. I was still deluded, thinking he was helpless in this situation, though there was so much evidence that he wasn't invested in me. I was gaslighting myself. I would remember nice things he did for me. I wished I could see him as a villain. If only I could hate him I could have moved on, I told myself. He was constantly in my head. I used to cry and pray I could meet him even for fifteen minutes. I used to keep glossing over everything and forgive him. In my head he could do nothing wrong. I used to feel I touched God.

One day I met an old friend from my MBA, one of our common friends, and suddenly she talked about Prabhakar. She mentioned that he had this Goa destination wedding and I was like no. She showed me her invite. And then I was like 'I've been crying my eyes out over him the last nine months.'

Until then I hadn't been able to hate Prabhakar. From that point on, slowly other things started making sense. For example, initially I had lots of friends at my MBA, then slowly they started vanishing. I couldn't understand why. Everyone knew I was dating Prabhakar. Only much later I realised he'd tell them I was busy. They would hang out without me, even have movie nights. He'd manipulated my friends to isolate me.

I went into my antisocial phase. I questioned what being around people was doing for me. I no longer wanted to text anyone or stay in touch. I think ultimately, I started liking my own company. In my head a metaphor started to grow. I would think of it as 'I'm just falling' and all these people who'd come into my life along the way were branches. But my feet were not on the ground.

And because I was afraid that I'd fall, I was holding on to the passing branches. This time I thought, 'Ok, so let me fall,' and that's how I found my own ground.

I'm better now at validating my feelings or entertaining myself. I realised I had my own voice after all. Except that until then, in all those anxieties, I never got to hear it. I've realised it's more reliable too – my own voice.

The good news I also wanted to share with you is – I'm getting married. It's an arranged marriage with a guy called Raghav. I'm not scared that it will break up. I like him but I don't love him. I realize I'm stronger and I don't need him to validate me in any way. I don't see him as a branch. I feel grounded in general. So, the stress on the relationship is less. He's dated a lot less women and his experience as a boyfriend is much less. Prabhakar was ten years older than me and came with a lot of skill and experience. Raghav isn't anywhere like that. He's more anxious than me. I like the newness of it for him. We had to talk about it a lot, even on affirming and validating myself. There are areas where I feel he compliments me well. For example, my relationship with my parents hasn't exactly been smooth. So, when I feel intense emotions, Raghav is more balanced, and if I can't judge or decide properly, he's reliable. Yet I'm very clear he's not a branch.

I'm enjoying being my own ground.

7

Which heartbreak pain trumps which? Is there a hierarchy in pain?

Remember the famous detergent ad that said, '*Bhala uski kameez meri kameez se zyaada safed kaise?*' How is his shirt whiter than mine? Marketeers are smart. They often tap into 'envy' to sell a product because most of us harbour a secret feeling that we are imposters, pretending to be cool and confident, but deep within, we feel like we're not good enough, good things aren't meant for us, that life chose us as the ones always destined for failure. We envy someone else who we think always had it easier compared to us. How many times have you met someone who barely listens to your *dukh bhari dastan* (sad story)? They can't wait for you to finish what you're saying, so they can jump in with 'That's nothing compared to what I went through!' If we're honest, we've probably been like that person too and thought things like that at some point. A colleague could be celebrated for delivering great work despite having a new born baby, but in our head we may be thinking, 'It's easy for them. They don't have the kind of spouse/in-laws/nightmare/controlling mother/high-handed father/landlord issues/zero help/ *phateechar* (pathetic) bank balance/demanding parent/ commitments at home like I had. Then we'd see how he/she could have delivered such great work.'

Basically, even when it comes to the losing game, we want to win at it. We award ourselves the invisible medal of 'my heartache pain is the heaviest of all!' This need to mentally compare and rank yourself 'the champion of all losers' is just self-defeating.

For a minute, think of heartbreak out of the romantic context. Imagine someone who just lost a young son in a military mission. Maybe he was the only child, or the only bread-winner, or the only one in the family to have broken away from farming. Can anyone compare that pain with say someone else whose child died by suicide? Does it matter that one person's child died one way and another's child died in another?

Or imagine a situation where someone lost a close family member overnight to a sudden, massive cardiac arrest. They never got to say goodbye, never imagined they would be returning home without them from the hospital. Can this be compared with the grief of another family where someone has lived a highly compromised life for very long because of a debilitating, incurable illness. Their grief is about a very prolonged, heart-wrenching goodbye with no relief or end in sight.

Which pain do you think is greater? Is there a greater-than or lesser-than way to view heartache?

Let's look at some heartbreak pains that are considered the worst and least of them all.

The first cut is the deepest. Is it?

There's a popular Rod Stewart song, 'The first cut is the deepest'. I'd hear that song and wonder, 'Is it really? Is it just a glamorisation of first love?' All those enchanting 'pehla pehla pyaar hai' (first love) songs sure made it feel like first love is incomparable. When I started looking for true stories of heartbreak, I would invariably be directed to stories of a first love – the one that was doomed from the start. In those stories, even decades later, the person was consumed with an aching wistfulness. Like the pain of losing the one they couldn't have was still such a heavy load that he/she carried in their hearts.

Especially if the person you couldn't end up with *wasn't* a jerk. It was *zaalim duniya* (cruel world) that came between both of you! That's a tough one to move on from. It's your classic Romeo-Juliet, Salim-Anarkali story. Two lovers that the world kept apart for external factors like class, caste or religious differences (as in the story 'Flights of fancy', we see Tarika comparing every relationship with her first boyfriend, Jude, who she didn't want to fight with her family to be with. She made him the benchmark, her lifelong reference point on romantic gestures. No other lover could match it. In such scenarios, the loss becomes even more glorified because it's the first time you experience all the chemical lochas, the euphoria of love. *Of course* everyone has to fall short, because they were not that first love and cannot replace what those first-ever emotions felt like. *That first experience, those first emotions of romance become the holy grail. Something that can never be reached or replicated.* But our stories show that more often than not, that feeling cannot be revisited with the same fire again. Not even if you met that person later in life and had a chance to re-open that door. In 'Flights of fancy', decades later when Tarika briefly went down that road with Jude again, she described it as 'yuck'. In 'The bigger picture', Vijay carried a torch for Bela for a long time. But when he did meet her once much later, and they had sex then for the first time, he still knew he wouldn't be repeating it again; and hasn't.

And what if that first person you gave a hundred per cent of yourself to turned out to be an asshole? Maybe you discovered he had ghosted or dumped you, been multi-timing and cheating on you. (As in 'Mentor tormentor'.) Or that he was in it for the short term, the fun and games, but wasn't willing to commit to what it might take to be with you. (As in 'Mirrors can lie' where we saw Raminder go all in with Joginder but he wasn't ready to accept his sexual identity and the decisions it would involve.) An experience that is doubly complicated like that wouldn't just be shattering; it would make it even more difficult to trust again.

Friends to lovers: It floats like a butterfly and stings like a bee

The promise of a partner who is also your best friend is intoxicating. Someone to share everything with, someone who *gets* you without explanation. When it works, nothing is sweeter than to go from being best friends to lovers; from being confidantes as friends to whispering sweet nothings as lovers. It can make for a dizzying romantic high. With the potential for a spectacular drop from those heights. Those who've gone through this will know that initial 'too good to be true' feeling. You already knew this person. You had seen them at their worst and their best. There was a history of shared jokes, an understanding of each other's quirks and vulnerabilities. This wasn't some shiny, new, exciting but also scary stranger; they felt safe. You both probably already had deep conversations; you had an emotional intimacy, you thought. What could be better than taking that to physical intimacy? While the going is good, it can't get any better than this. But that's only as long as it works.

The fallout: A double whammy

When a 'friends to lovers' relationship turns sour, you don't just lose a lover, you lose your friend too. That's a biggie. The loss of two important relationships! The comfort you both once shared is gone, or at best is strained. This heartbreak is a hard one to recover from, for sure. From people I spoke to who had been through this, problems begin with the blurring of boundaries. Friendship and romance have different rules and unspoken agreements. What was acceptable as a friend (teasing, blunt honesty) might feel hurtful or inappropriate in a romantic context. Simple situations suddenly become fraught with egos, tricky navigation and often resentment. When a 'friends to lovers' relationship goes wrong, it becomes a helluva lot more emotionally loaded than a regular break-up. Like, 'how could *you*?' It stings more because we thought that person knew us so well. And yet, *they* let us down. The chances of going back to being good friends become pretty low.

The loss doesn't end there: This kind of break-up is an almost-divorce. You're splitting 'assets' like mutual friends, places you went to together. All the stuff that felt familiar and good, feels like a minefield to be navigated now. You go through grief seeing common friends pick sides and have to choose which friends, interests, places you want to avoid, maybe even lose. In 'February 13th, 14th or 15th', Trixie tells us about one of her main regrets about dating and breaking up with her best friend Shaurya, which led to everyone else staying friends while she lost the whole group she had grown up with in Toronto. So much of pop culture has played out storylines in this 'friends to lovers' break-up scenario *because* of how many people can relate to it. Remember the *Friends* gang after Ross and Rachel's millionth break-up? Suddenly, loyalties got messy. Group hangouts required insane juggling. And as for trying to go back to being friends. That's a no-brainer. We saw this in Mihika's story, 'Friends and lovers'.

The pain of an 'almost-relationship': Why does it hurt so much if you barely dated?

What about someone who had a brief, undefined relationship with someone? What if there was nothing 'official' yet about the two of you but for one person, the attachment was very strong, very real. Ambiguity actually intensifies grief. The lack of real-time interaction and clarity is a sure way for endless projection. When the other person doesn't define what the relationship is, or where things stand, you build castles in the air, without labels, without restraints. The almost-relationship heartbreak is grieving not just the person but the potential of what could have been and all the hope placed on that imagined future. If friends tell you you're over-reacting, *you are absolutely not. There wasn't clarity.* So your brain filled in the blanks. No one said you shouldn't go there. But you did. And when that almost-relationship crashed, it left you feeling stupid. By what logic should that not hurt? Your pain is as legit as anyone else's.

So which heartbreak pain is the greatest of all?

There is no greater-than or lesser-than value to say which kind of heartbreak situation trumps which. A relationship that was made formal with roka-shoka done or one that was forbidden or a long-distance one or a long live-in relationship or an almost-relationship? Who is to say 'why are you crying over *that*?'

Which heartbreak pain is the toughest one of them all? The answer is – the one that you are going through.

Friends and lovers: Mihika's story

I was seventeen, Michael was eighteen. We were part of the same circle of friends; my brother and he were good friends too. I don't know when we went from being friends to best friends. He was Christian, the youngest of five siblings. In the 90s, there were no malls in Chandigarh. The group had innocent fun. At a house party 'truth or dare', I discovered Michael had a crush on me. It changed the dynamic between us. I became aware of him and the way he would look at me. It was understood that Michael and I would start dating. When people would plan parties, they started putting our names, Michael and Mihika, together in one line.

We were both private people. We had similar tastes in music and loved dogs madly. My parents weren't averse to dogs, but I couldn't bring strays home. Michael was constantly rescuing them and taking them to his home. I would hang out at his place, caring for the newest rescues with him. We didn't care about getting our hands dirty and cleaning up some of the sad, abandoned dogs, putting them into an auto, taking them to the Government vet nearby, caring for our scared and wounded little fur babies and bringing them back to good health. There was no specific moment when the friendship started turning into love, but there was a high understated tone of passion that we hadn't yet given into. He was a staunch Christian and claimed that the person he ended up with had to be a 'believer'. He felt that he couldn't lead me on and that always put the brakes on him.

At eighteen, I wanted to live in the present. We still had to go to college. There was a lot of life ahead, a lot of figuring out to do. I wasn't holding back my feelings for him, while his faith was short-circuiting his brain. A lot of this, I figured out only later. I could see him pulling back from me. There was so much unsaid – and not giving in to the need to be freely and fully with each other romantically. I would feel hurt that he was ignoring what I wanted – to be 'us'. We still talked a lot all the time. It mattered to me that we stayed friends as the relationship moved into romance. He wasn't great academically and flunked a year. I was his counsel when he got into college in Chennai. In my third year, my dad passed away. Michael was a big support. He came down to Chandigarh, used up a chunk of his savings to buy the ticket. Around then we also decided to move to Chennai. Again, Michael was a big help, with my brother's admission and with helping mom settle in. To me, it meant a lot. I was hoping we'd 'reconnect'.

In Chandigarh, he was practically a saint. In Chennai, he'd changed – constantly experimenting with booze, drugs, ciggies. My hopes to get more time together in Chennai were dashed. It felt like I was always chasing and asking him to make time to be with me. It was a rough period for my family – moving from the North to the South, that too to such a slow city, and with a lot of financial pressures. In my 20s, I never thought of marriage. My parents didn't pressure me. Dad wanted me to be financially independent and I wanted to make sure I honoured that. I decided to skip postgrad for a year. Michael was still in college and I had started working. Again, we were in different phases.

I had always seen two main male figures in my life, Dad and Michael. The heartache kept resurfacing, dealing with losing dad and then Michael, who was there but not there. The larger heartbreak was in losing my friend, someone close to me, not just a former love. I was so lonely in those three or four years which passed. Michael was my first love. I don't know if he realised it. It hurt a lot. He finished college and decided to go to Pilani for postgrad. After I had saved to do my post-grad, I moved to Bangalore. By then my desire, intensity, and need for him had dwindled. You don't realize that you are healing all the time.

One day in 2014, weirdly, he drunk-dialled me. He asked if by any chance we could rekindle what we had. I don't know what was going on in his head. By then I was like, 'Whaaat?' Spiritually he had been so strong, taken me to his church, I met his church friends over the years. Now, he had cut away from his entire church group; not that he had cut away from the entire friends' group that we were part of. For me, any relationship has been shaped by what I had with Michael – an intellectual, emotional and beautiful physical connection with someone with a great value system. And his sense of humour – my parents loved it too.

Back when we were friends, he was always everybody's advisor, the upright guy who knew what to do. That dynamic started changing in Chennai when I became his go-to person for advice. From best friend, to his love, to turning agony aunt, I'd tell myself at least I've gone from being needy to being needed again. It was my temporary balm, a kind of catharsis while I tried holding on to him as a friend. I knew losing him as a friend would hurt even more than losing him as a spouse, which is what he had been in my heart earlier. But it didn't help in any way. This one-sided effort into keeping our friendship going would sting me and haunt me. Clearly it wasn't enough for him. He was the one who finally chose to distance himself and move away from me.

Earlier, if we went to each other's city, we'd meet up. Over the years everything dwindled. His cool statement like, 'Why should it matter to you if I don't call?' left me sobbing one night. I kept crying that he wasn't there for me. In that call at least, he acknowledged it. 'Even this friendship has sustained because of you. It's you that kept it going for so long.'

I kept pining for him. It affected all my other relationships. With friends, relatives – I felt anger. With Michael I felt deeply sad. I regretted that I allowed our friendship to go down the path of love.

In his head, we still had a friendship. In my head, both our relationships had ended. The love, gone; the friendship also gone.

Now we don't even wish each other on our birthdays. We haven't met in many years. At least our reconnection brought me back in touch with his friends, which continued.

The first cut is the deepest, but I tell myself, from that heartbreak I have new friends. Including a new guy friend who is almost like I have a reincarnated friend in him. We are so close; we tell each other it's like I have a penis and he has a vagina. It feels that safe.

There are so many levels on which I miss Michael.

He's married; he changed his church, but he's so private that no one knows what happened.

He didn't even message me he had a baby. Now he's a ghost, a stranger to me.

That painful time led to a lot of frustration and jealousy. I realised that if he wanted to cut away, then chuck it. Meanwhile, in my life too, the voids are filled by many things. I work in the policy space, with a big think-tank. I have my social circle.

After dating him I didn't date anyone for seven years. You can try, try, try, but sometimes the circuit in your brain says 'enough, now stop'. I got perspective on the years in Chennai. From pinning my hopes on being where my best friend was, to seeing that he was not pedestal worthy. He was messed up and not interested in getting help. Michael was constantly stoned, getting drunk; he even lost a job, because he'd keep landing up drunk to work. I started feeling glad that I didn't end up with him. I've always lived in moderation. To think that at eighteen he was giving me lectures on drinking. People who try to be Mr Fixit are often broken inside. They like to have this exterior of power and control but they're often messed up inside.

One big change that happened for me, was getting my mother to be more accepting towards rescuing dogs, which really matters to me. I accept that I can't bring them all home, but my current dog, Jalebi, is a rescue.

I love her to bits. I only meet friends at places which are pet-friendly.

I don't want to 'settle' by just marrying anyone. In any case, I think marriage is not a must. I strongly believe if a woman needs a man in her life, he must add value.

Now my benchmarks are many. Maybe he was the bedrock but after him, there were others. The difference is, I've learned to set boundaries. In all my relationships, not just with guys, by learning that it's ok to let go. I know when to spot red flags now, like when a guy is too dominating or shows a narcissistic streak or is less interested than you are. I've learned to communicate and teach people how to treat me. I know when to walk out.

One of the guys I dated had a horrible temper. I couldn't handle it and said so. Then the guy learned. He would take a walk if his anger was getting out of check. Also, people who are flaky – if they give me a time and don't keep to it, I'm clear now that I'm not ok with it. I give any person one chance and no more.

Earlier I used to be scared of saying things like 'Well then, we need to move on,' or 'let's go our separate ways.' Now, without any hesitation, I say it. Men think women aren't serious when they say something like that. Then they realize I mean it. What's the worst that can happen? That I'll stay single. That I'll come home after work to mom and Jalebi. Maybe I'll meet someone, or maybe I won't. It doesn't sound all that bad a life to me at all.

Mirrors can lie: Raminder's story

∞

My problem is I'm only attracted to toxic Punjabi men. Another thing, I've never actually had a break-up. Things go bad, things repair themselves, but the only person breaking up is me, on the inside.

I am a woman trapped in a man's body. I was born Raminder Kalra, but in my head I was always a Rama. A hot, intelligent Rama who didn't tolerate any nonsense from men who were jerks. Men who were solid studs, with good futures – those were the only kind I would give any bhav to. How is that ever going to work for me, when the world only sees Raminder, a quiet, handsome mard?

Joginder – the guy who broke me up probably doesn't even realize it. I was in Jalandhar, studying literature; he was studying engineering in the same college. Of course, I'd seen him around campus. He was a hunk, just stunning and sexy, like God made him on his best day ever. Not before and not since then have I seen perfection in every line in a man's body. I was madly attracted to him. I had no idea he even knew of my existence. He must have made enquiries for sure because he made the first move. He contacted me on WhatsApp and asked me to help him write his English assignment. I knew I'd do it. I am not just a looker; there is a lot up there also. In no time, I worked on 400 pages. When he came to collect his assignment, was the first time we really looked at each other. After that we had our first phone call. I remember all these milestones, all these dates, frankly even the timings that all these things happened.

I used to beg him to video-call me – just so that I could see his face. I lovvvved every inch of it. He used to be so tender, so charming, never in a hurry to go anywhere if we were on a call. When we would be hanging out together, he would always hug, a lingering hug where I knew that he was also attracted to me. Even the way his beautiful stubble would brush against my cheek, there was so much that was unspoken, but it was there. Oh yes, I'm not an idiot. *Aag toh dono taraf se hai, ab barabar hai ya nahi?* (There's definitely a spark on both sides. But is it equal or not?) I used to wonder. In my dreams we could say the things that I think he also was thinking. I would speak openly with him in my journal. He was the reason I could look in the mirror and imagine he saw the beauty in me. The woman within me that the mirror couldn't reflect. Mirrors are superficial. I hoped he saw that.

Then out of nowhere, he told me he was leaving for Canada. That the paperwork had taken ages but it finally worked out and he wanted to put Jalandhar and India behind him. Within days he flew off to Canada. I felt shattered. I removed him from my WhatsApp. Soon after, I received a follow request from him on Insta. I accepted it even though I was pained; his actions didn't match his words. Why? Was I part of what he wanted to forget about India? Then why connect after reaching Canada? I started watching all his Insta stuff. It was clear he slept around with women too. His online stuff made me so jealous. Till then we were DMing each other, he was saying I should visit him in Canada. But just looking at his Insta made me so sick, so angry, that nine months ago I texted him that he couldn't have his cake and eat it too. I called it off. I guess you can say out of revenge and haughtiness. Now I go over this again and again.

My relationship, love affair, some might say unrequited love, though I don't think so, no, he definitely gave me a hell of a lot of reason to believe it was love for both of us; call it what you like, lasted two years. Back then I was 21, now I am 27. My heart was so connected with his that I used to really feel as if he was my life partner. I used to take myself out for a treat on his birthday. I would go and feed the poor in Jalandhar on his birthday. He said, 'I'll always be there for you.' Then how could he flaunt other women in my face?

This relationship was a watershed moment for me. Till then I felt disconnected from my reflection in the mirror. It took me months of grieving, reading, listening to Punjabi songs, making my space, my identity in a place like Jalandhar.

Initially, I'd keep latching on to something. Like I went through hours of learning about skin care. I perfected looking after my skin and built myself on this front. Then after another heartbreak after my darling Jogi, I went crazy about colouring my hair. If a guy initiated a break-up with me, I'd keep asking people who was better looking, me or him? If they said it was the guy, I would get so jealous, so upset, so focused on looking for ways to prove them wrong. I'd look for ways to get reassurance that I could do without this guy. It may not be the most ideal graph in terms of my own journey and what I wanted from relationships. But I have become quite a big social media influencer.

I look for ways to get reassurance from my Insta following that I can do without whoever the latest guy is. I have many friends, including ciggy-kiosk hijras and migrant workers. They are cool with me. I get their honest opinions. Facts are facts. I live in Punjab, and here everyone is obsessed with looks. In my experience, in Punjab, love is more about looks and assets than about emotions or feelings.

Jogi never told me he is bi. Every guy I start liking turns out to be straight. I continue caring about them, crying over them, and listening to Punjabi songs. Of late I feel that even when I turn 50, I'll tell others, especially my Insta followers and especially young girls, that they should hate men maybe. I'm going to tell them a hard truth that people hardly ever share. I'll tell them all that men are not creatures to feel for or to love. Sleep with them by all means, it's a bodily need, but to all, I would say 'men are not reliable'.

I spit on the attitude of most macho men, who think housework is women's work and below their dignity. I clean my own dishes, do my own laundry. I want to rid myself of all the toxic traits that Indian men, especially Punjabi men have. For some time, I even took to following a guru and doing meditation, but I'll be honest, it did nothing for me.

If a good-looking guy sends me a Facebook request, it's still never simple for me, even if I'm attracted to him. I don't know when I'll work Jogi out of my system.

How I had made him the centre of my life, and to him I was so disposable. Even when I think I'm in love with another guy, I can't forget Jogi.

Two years ago, I also started working as a lecturer at a liberal arts college. Jogi comes from a village close to Hoshiarpur. If I show my students pictures of Joginder and any student says they've seen him, that student becomes my favourite. That's how much of a soft spot I still have for my Jogi, even though it's over. *Sabko social media bemari hi ho gai hai* (everyone's got the social media addiction), to keep scrolling, to keep feeling sad at what we know is the reality of our lives, and keep envying people who look happy. It makes me sick and angry, but I still have a nightly ritual of scrolling through Joginder's feed. Sometimes I wish I hadn't deleted him from WhatsApp, because I still keep yearning to get information about him. I keep asking a female friend if he's changed his WhatsApp DP or what's on his WhatsApp updates.

I started hanging out more with my queer friends to meet more like-minded people, but for them I'm still a minority. They treat me as a gay boy, but I want them to treat me as a pretty girl, buy me pretty and expensive *salwar* suits with glittering *dupatta*s. I dream that their mums will treat me like a *bahu* (daughter-in-law). Now that I've started being much more open about what I identify as, I post about some of the shit I've been through. Many are fascinated by me. They see me as a role model.

Recently I was at a protest with some of my queer friends. One of them introduced me to this guy, Mandeep.

He was all over me with compliments and left with my number. I've seen enough guys by now to know he was instantly attracted. One picks up the vibe. He drunk calls, drunk texts me. I've been down this road before. He thinks he loves me, he's the first to view my Insta stories so he can't be confused that I'm gay. My friend says he asks about me all the time. His texts would make any woman's head swoon and be fooled into thinking that he's the one who will overcome all odds to be with me. But I know that this too will be like a soda, it'll fall flat soon after I open the bottle and imagine there's a future for me with any man. I know in my heart that Mandeep too will finally take the safe way out, give in to his family's expectations and marry a woman. Part of me feels sad at becoming cynical.

While I continue to build my public persona as a sorted trans woman, I keep torturing myself by not breaking contact with Joginder. He still keeps DM-ing me. Those disappearing DMs. Why? Why not comment on my Insta in a public way? You tell me. Obviously, he wants to have his cake and eat it too. To keep me in his life to boost his ego, as a popular social media influencer ka *adhoora* (incomplete) love – the one guy I could never get over. So many times, he's asked me to come to Canada to meet him. I think about it often. I don't want to go there on his invitation. I want to build a huge following, go on my own steam, wear sarees there and be an icon for people like me. I want to casually run into Joginder and have his children come and tell me that they are my fans. But that's just one scenario I play out. As far as I know, Joginder is still not married.

Nobody's allowed to talk to me about his marriage. My heart will stop the day that happens.

More and more I have started trying to embrace the reality that I can be single for life. Why do I have to keep imagining and then cancelling on my dreams of a future with a man. I look at role models of single people who are living fulfilling lives. I start feeling, 'If Arundhati Roy can live as a single person, why can't I?' It's only lately that I can face the mirror and feel a little comfortable with the reflection I see. I see Rama emerging, minus the obsessions about skin, hair, looks. Well, mirrors are fragile; and they can be such liars. I know better than to trust them. I look at myself in the mirror but don't linger. I have to look beyond the reflection.

8

It is what it is. It is over

I'm sorry to have to do this, but someone needs to hold up a mirror to show you what you keep refusing to see. There you were calling and texting the former love of your life yet again to tell them about something aggravating, in the hope it would start your chats again. Let's say an asshole hit your vehicle. You tried calling that still-special-to-you person to vent about it. But they didn't pick up the call. You texted them about the whole drama. You thought you'd see a reply when they woke up, be upset on your behalf. But, WTF, they didn't even text you back! Not last night. Not this morning. Not all day. And it is not as if they were caught up with some crisis. Because you saw that they were reposting things on social media. You saw them online for a long time too. They couldn't find a minute all day to reply to your text? You really think it's because they are too busy? Please. Wake up.

Read between the lines. No message is a message too.

Let's give this a try. Dearest Nisha/ Nishant/ insert your name. There you were, waiting for them to look your way, to show you some attention, but they didn't. Or maybe they sent some throwaway text like 'Ohho' or 'Bummer'. It was not at all the loving response you were hoping for. And you know, if that darling of yours had wanted to do it, it wouldn't have taken more than a minute to show they cared. They did not. Instead, you had them dominate your thoughts all day, barely able to function, hoping they would call, maybe even land up.

Face it. *They could have done it but they didn't. It is what it is.*

The sooner you stop brushing aside how it has been playing out with this person you are crying over, no matter how witty or intelligent or body-positive or brilliant in bed they are, the sooner you will realise the truth. That this supposed soulmate is not really invested in you. You are low on their priorities. They throw you sporadic scraps of affection to keep you interested. You made them a priority but you are an option for them. I'm so sorry, I know it hurts. But clearly, they are not invested; even if they are kinda, sorta showing that they are interested, and only sometimes. You've been eagerly and generously giving your time and attention to them on a platter, in return for a few crumbs of affection! Why?!! Why stick around at a table where respect for your feelings isn't being served!

How many more ways can I say this to you? It's time to say goodbye.

Even if it was good once. Even if, at one time in the relationship, there was fantastic energy, sparks and chemistry that was sooo good to feel. But that's not the scene anymore. It changed.

It went flat. They went silent. Or cold. Whatever. Or worse, maybe you went into it a hundred per cent committed. But the person showed themselves to be a narc or an abuser. Yet you stayed. Thinking this was something that had lasted a long time. You couldn't quit, for the kids. Or, because you kept hoping they would change. Or, because you have trauma bonding and didn't even know what that was and how you too could have responded differently. And have only just reached a point where you realise you can't live this tortured life any more.

Meanwhile, it's quite possible they don't care if you're crying your heart out. Yes? So stop investing more of yourself in a person who never valued your precious heart. Okay? It is time to say a hard 'enough' and mentally say 'Ta-Ta, bye bye'. And no, you don't need more drama of saying an actual goodbye. They don't deserve that satisfaction. If at all you need to vent, draft a text/mail first. Keep it crisp and keep your dignity.

I beg you to take your 'in love' blinkers off and see it for what it is.

It is over. The reason I am hammering on about this is because you can't progress until you accept what it is. FINITO. They knew you would have stayed. They chose to leave.

They were not inconsistent. They were in fact consistently showing you who they were.

You just kept hoping they'd change. If you're honest with yourself, you'll realise that you are not just heartbroken over them, but also over all the future scenarios you had built for the two of you together – all of which came crashing down with the break-up. You are grieving the loss of what could have been. The potential they never lived up to. And which your relationship could never fulfil. So all your grieving over them wasn't really about you chasing your one big love. You were (maybe) chasing validation from someone who could not even give you clarity (that's for sure!) Stop replaying the good moments. That version of them only showed up when it served them.

It is not so confusing. You were just giving extra meaning to things that weren't real.

You are the main character in this. Close the chapter that isn't serving your story.

No one else matters more than you. That person moved on. Friends went on with their lives. I'm willing to bet some friends even picked sides and you lost them with the relationship. Others are avoiding you and your gloom because that's just how they are. Make a mental note of the fair-weather friends and the ones who stayed with you through this time. They care; they want to be there for you. But here you are, still stuck in feeling rejected. It's like the tyres of a vehicle that went into a soft *khud-da* (slushy hole) in wet mud. That tyre is your mind going round and round, rehashing your story of pain. It needs someone to help push that vehicle out of its stuck groove. That someone is me, telling you to get this burned into your brain. Whether or not you told them about your feelings, your actions towards them said what you felt. And that you wanted it to play out differently.

They knew your feelings. But they chose to let you go. That is their choice, their loss.

This story is about you. Your sanity, your peace, your being able to get past this. This is the part where I need you to say 'Bahut ho gaya, ENOUGH,' to what is already in the past.

How dare you give your main-character power over to somebody who wasn't there for you? Who isn't making any genuine effort to show you that you mean a lot to them. No matter how good they were once, no matter how special it felt when it was good, *now it is about you.* And let me tell you, in any good script, any important decision in the story can't come from someone else. That change has to come from you. Bring your main-character energy back in your story.

It takes two to make a relationship work. Both must want to.

We keep putting so much of ourselves into making things work, even with friends and family. That feeling of 'I tried and tried and yet for this person, even my best wasn't enough' is horrible. We put the entire onus of making something work on ourselves. Why? Low self-esteem for one. We think something is lacking in us, *mujhme hi kuch hai* (there's something about me), that screws everything up. We seek *confirmation bias* (there's something about me). Like, if you're convinced you drive people away, the break-up becomes another brick in the wall to cement that thought.

We also tend to make ourselves even more miserable with *emotional reasoning. We believe something is true because we feel it to be true,* a conclusion based on emotion, rather than on objective reasons. Like, 'I feel like a failure, so I must be one.' (Never mind that I just got a promotion/improved my fitness, etc.) And then there's our conditioning! (Our parents/ society/films all play their part!) We think a relationship hangs on things that we grew up thinking matter. Things like our attractiveness, our honesty, our loyalty, our ability to provide for them, our ability to host beautiful parties, our anticipating their every need and prioritising them. These things alone did not and will not guarantee a person stays in a relationship. The commitment that has to come from them is not in your hands. *Doh haath se taali bajti hai.* (It takes two hands to clap).

When a person wants to stay: they'll fight for you and the relationship.

The only way to *keep* a partner is if they genuinely want to be kept by you. If the person is truly committed, they'll fight for you and the relationship. Nothing can fake or force the desire to stay. If they aren't fighting for you when things get tough, it's a clear sign they are no longer invested in the relationship. Mentally they have already tuned out. *See the signs and accept it. You can't force love. Know when to let go.*

A painful realization I came to is that just because you gave someone love, it is not written in any rule book that it'll be reciprocated. The same is true for respect. You can't force either of these things from anyone. Either it is there or it isn't. And honestly, it has little to do with what you put into it. More importantly, it doesn't mean that you are unloveable or unworthy of respect. That ability to love you just wasn't there *in them.* Or it changed at some point. What can you do about it? NOTHING. If they valued being with you, in the relationship, they would have put some effort into communicating (not gaslighting), into listening as well as talking, into working through whatever became a dealbreaker for them.

This isn't about you giving up on them; it's the other way around. They have given up. *It's crucial that you stop wasting any more of your valuable time.* Look, they lost the privilege of being a part of your life when they chose a path that didn't include you. At least now, walk away.

Between a rock and a hard place: Nilima's story

I'm Nilima Ajani, 38 years old and single.

I've had two serious relationships in my life and some not-serious ones, which I won't get into. The first one, with Viraj, ended eleven years ago. I met him in Delhi, at my first event management job. In event management you pretty much spend your life working insane hours. I was twenty-two, fresh out of college. He was already a name in the business, had risen shockingly fast, won an impressive amount of industry awards already. I was lucky to have been put in his group. The stories around him were the stuff of legend – his biting sarcasm with dumb account executives bearing shiite briefs. He was also known to be fair to his team, giving credit, giving a chance to travel to the big events if their work got through. I considered myself lucky when he started singling me out for some important projects. I would bask in his praise if he liked my ideas. It was common for folks to head out for a drink after a late night of work. Soon Viraj and I would end up sitting closer, the chemistry became apparent to everybody in the group. The dating got serious and I didn't doubt that he was into me, but there were things that left me confused. For example, the regular partying led to my gaining weight. It wasn't in anything he said, but the way he'd look at me, made me feel like I was being judged by him.

My mother is a single, divorced woman. She has been bipolar for as long as I can remember and I ended up becoming her main caregiver. Home was never really welcoming, or homey. I never knew what I was walking back into. I had hoped that Viraj was thinking about us in terms of marriage, but he was just not showing keenness. What had earlier been fun, witty, animated, sparky outings had changed into lecture sessions about how I should be focusing more on work and getting some weight off. His career was on the up-and-up and he saw no reason to not enjoy it all fully.

Ideation work is largely sedentary. My weight gain didn't help either. Before I knew it, I had developed a disc problem. I was twenty-nine by then and starting to give up all hope of anything changing as far as Viraj was concerned in making our relationship serious. In desperation, at first, to try and get back in shape and to win him back and less because of the constant pain with my slipped disc, I quit event management. To focus on getting fit.

Viraj was supportive – but I felt him becoming more and more distant. He was always in the middle of a big presentation. I knew how it worked; I wasn't doubting him but it started whittling down to occasional phone calls. He would ask how I was doing and repeat that I should take care of my back problem. I knew his mother didn't like me. I also knew that she thought I was too independent. She always acted surprised if I said things like 'We all wrapped up at 3 a.m. last night.' She asked if I saw myself doing this all my life (which I definitely read as whether I intended to work after marriage/ kids too). I said, 'Of course, Aunty.'

I had been open about my background with Viraj. I think maybe he shared it with his mother too. I knew that she was an old-fashioned woman; in their family women don't work. More important, I don't think she quite understood anything about mental health or cared to have a daughter-in-law whose parents were divorced. I tried to stay in touch with Viraj initially, at least to hold on to him as a friend but that didn't work.

It wasn't a pleasant period in my life. Luckily for me, my back healed. My heart didn't. I had a few flings on the rebound in the hope that it would give me the high I needed to pull myself out of the depression of losing both the guy I loved and the job I loved. I considered going back to that company.

Call it bad timing or good, there was no opening for someone at my level. I decided to focus on getting into better shape. It was also a way I could keep my depression at bay. I don't think I had ever really got over the way Viraj had smoothly extricated himself from our relationship. I saw my fitness obsession initially as a kind of beautiful revenge, to get back to looking hot and then run into him. But our worlds just didn't overlap.

It was practically like a 'no contact' situation. Slowly, unintentionally, I moved on.

The second guy in my life was Denzel. I met him at a friend's Holi party. I was working with another company by then. Denzel was working with a big sports brand, in marketing. His company insisted that every employee had to go through fitness training. By that time, I had become a fitness trainer, taking weekend Zumba classes. It gave me balance in my life.

My mother's bipolar issues had got aggravated. There were frequent spikes and a lot of stress, and emergency visits to see her doctor. It left me feeling quite low too because I'm also bipolar; luckily, mine is borderline. I found that the only way I can handle my bipolar issues is to recognise that I don't do well with being idle. So, the moment I find myself getting to that place, I'm off to the gym and work out like crazy.

Denzel and I became very serious, very fast. In just a few months I moved into his house. It was a good arrangement because it got me away from mom and home but kept me in the same city to be ready to rush to her help at any sign of a crisis. It was only when Denzel and I started living together that I realised he had serious depression. He would keep disappearing completely or keep skipping meds for the way it clouded his brain; also, though he wouldn't say it, because it affected his libido. It became a double trauma for me, to try and find him and talk to him and get him to come back home. And it would only sharply remind me of all the times that I had been taking care of mom. I started feeling stuck – as if there was just no escaping this in my life. Her mental health, his mental health, my mental health – it would really get to me. For all the good we were, and we were so compatible; yet, his depression would be back, despite the meds, the docs, the support from his company, and despite all the love that I tried to give him.

Who would know better than me that it was not about

me? The depression was part of him but it became more and more difficult for me to live with it. By now we had been living together for about three years. My career in event management had become more an on-off affair. Fitness training was the only good constant relationship I had going for myself.

In the third year of our living together, at a party in Gurgaon, Denzel told me that he'd decided he should go back to Amsterdam. He would speak to his company. If they wouldn't agree, he would go back anyway and look for another job there. I started saying I would come with him. I broke down. I cried all night and begged him not to do it. I had already imagined our future together. I told him again and again, 'Denzo, don't go. Please don't go. We can deal with it.' His mind was completely closed. He was fixated on going away alone. He just kept saying you're doing too much for me already.

I couldn't believe that he chose to go back without me. Our relationship had been pretty solid. It was never about the games. In three years, we had broken up only once. Now I started feeling as if I had pushed him away with my pressure to take me with him to Amsterdam.

So, we parted ways then with the understanding that I would follow after some months to be with him. In that time, I moved back to my mother's. Fortunately, it was a stable period. She and I were comfortable with each other but there were too many memories of all the times I had been a caregiver to her. I was just exhausted from all of it. I kept crying over why I couldn't have someone in my life who could be there for me.

The reality of what was ahead, especially with Denzel's

mental health too, started feeling like a dead-end to me. It was only a few months later but felt like a lifetime by the time I went out to meet him in Amsterdam. When I went there, I realised that even though I had done all that I had for my mother, I didn't know if I had it in me anymore to do it for my boyfriend. He didn't work around his issues anymore. He seemed to have sunk into a further low. Even though I realised he needed my help, I asked myself, 'Can I do this? I don't feel loved.' In the long run it's only going to be tougher.

Being there with him, after the months apart, suddenly made everything crystal clear. Being with him didn't make me happy and I realised I can't make him happy. Only he could do that.

I went for a long walk while I was there. I had to make a tough choice. Caring for the man I loved or caring for myself, for the rest of my life. It felt so unfair. Why should it have to be that way? In the park I saw people jogging, couples sitting on benches, life going on busily, people sharing a laugh, or going about their lives, cycling purposefully – regardless of whether they were single or a couple. And then I asked myself the question: if the tables were turned, would he have looked after you, Nilima?

I had the answer to that.

I returned to India. Life continues to be a see-saw – looking after mom, myself, and dealing with the heaviness of living with my decision. A love that I chose to walk away from. And choosing myself.

9

Why does love change? Why did I not see it coming?

∞

We all keep trying to make sense of traumatic life events like it's a frustrating puzzle to be solved. I know I do. But there isn't always a logical answer to everything. In which case, I find it useful to stop trying so hard. I've always felt that sometimes we are reminded of things through messages in books or song lyrics or stories we hear, because they are meant for us at that exact point in time. I was fortunate to have two uncles who were both spellbinding storytellers. Both influenced my reading. A lot of it didn't 'make sense' then but later, when some of those stories resurfaced in a perfect, mystical way, they felt like 'Aha' answers to my questions.

Let me tell you a Zen story that I'd once read. It may give you clarity, now or a little later about the question: 'why does love change?'

A young monk tells an older monk that he feels that the person he loves is slipping away. He tells his mentor that where once he and his beloved walked together, they now walk apart. The old monk says to him, 'Love is like the morning mist upon the mountain. It is soft and serene. It seems eternal. Yet as the sun rises, as it must, the mist starts to go away. And we see the bare stone beneath it.' But in life when love leaves us, it doesn't vanish gently like mist. The naked landscape it exposes, the stripped-away feeling it leaves as its reality, feels unbearably harsh to bear. That mist over the mountains that represented love was never meant to be there for eternity.

Love, loss and letting go: The story of the falling leaves

The poor, young monk keeps weeping. Why did his love's behaviour change? He tells the old monk that he had noticed some subtle changes, but he ignored them initially. (Like the changed behaviours of so many of the exes in the stories in this book.) It was like the first leaf falling before autumn arrived. Then the young monk noticed more and more changes, like more leaves falling, till it became impossible to ignore. He asked the Zen master what he had done wrong. You see where I'm going with this? *'Why, why, why didn't I see it coming?'* is one of the biggest regrets when a relationship ends. We torture ourselves rehashing what we could have done differently. If only we had seen it coming, we could have stopped it.

Why do people who once looked at you with warmth suddenly look at you with indifference?

There's a Buddhist word called 'annica' which means 'change' or 'impermanence'. It is considered the fundamental truth of existence. Whether we like it or not, all things including emotions, relationships and attachments are going to change. The old monk says, 'Just as a river *never clings* to the banks of the places it passes, when someone loses their love for you, they don't announce it with great ceremony. Instead, they do two things to mark the death of what once was.'

When people lose love, they withhold their presence.

The old monk takes the young, heart-broken monk to a garden. There's a bird sitting on a branch, singing away happily. The monk waves his hand. The bird flies off. So the monk says, 'Look. Love is actually like that bird. When it was comfortable it lingered. It was singing. But when the bird sensed disturbance and something upset its equilibrium, it moved off.' The young monk is still upset. 'But why didn't they tell me?' He was thinking he'd have done anything to keep the bird with him. If only he had realised it wasn't happy. To which the older monk says, 'It's because they are still learning who they are, themselves.'

'So what should I do? Should I chase? Should I beg?' he asks. The old monk says, 'Would you chase the bird or beg the leaf not to fall?' The monk says no. It seems obvious when it comes to a bird that it must move away when it is no longer comfortable, doesn't it? But not so obvious when we beat ourselves up over a person whose emotional presence left us, the home, the relationship, much before they left physically. We need to remind ourselves that *when love withdraws, there is nothing to be achieved in chasing it. The only thing we can do, which honours us, is to honour the passage of that love you had.* Had. Note that we are accepting that it was there, but *it has passed. It is in the past.*

When love changes, the person becomes someone else.

The old monk takes the heartbroken young monk to a pond. He shows the young monk his reflection in it and then throws a stone in the pond. Lots of ripples are formed in the water. The water shifts and the reflection changes. The older monk explains it saying, 'The person who once laughed at your jokes has shifted form and already become someone else. You can't bring back the person you once loved because that person has already gone.'

Because our love shapes our identity, we grieve not only for lost love, but for the person they once were. And who we were with them. But we need to remember that the person we miss no longer exists. We see this in stories here like 'Friends and lovers' and also 'Slow burn'. The grieving is for all that the relationship *was*, how that person *was* with you, *before the change.*

From 'why', let's go to 'how': How does one bear such a loss?

It's normal to think of doing things like confronting or exposing the ex or posting accusative things about them or talking ill of them to everyone in common. *Why lose your dignity also, after already losing the relationship? The only thing any radioactive, reactive do, do, do will do, is do you harm.*

I remember coming out of a meeting once. I was walking towards my car when a man from the group started matching steps with me. I had heard his wife and he were going through serious issues. I knew them both but I didn't know either of them well enough to know details. Before I knew it, the man had launched into a vicious 'do you know' expose about his (soon-to-be) ex-wife. Of course I shut him down, but I couldn't help thinking as I left, that all the foul stuff that he had launched into, only reflected poorly on him, not on his wife, who kept her mouth zipped and dignity intact in the divorce to follow.

My life hack: When in doubt, do nothing.

Whenever I find myself stuck, when the choices are hard and I feel conflicted, I force myself to drag my feet. I make no impulsive decision and buy myself time. I tell myself, *'When in doubt, do nothing.'* You'd be surprised how many things become clearer or more settled if we *force ourselves to put temporary brakes on our impulse to act and act NOW.* Instead of NOW, tell yourself NO.

Disclaimer: At no time do I suggest doing nothing when you're in a stuck place in the relationship or being disrespected or feeling like something's got to give. In all such situations, do whatever you need to. Get therapy, get space, get couple counselling if there is scope for mending, or get away to protect yourself.

I propose the 'Do nothing' mantra ONLY when the relationship is already over. When you are consumed by raging emotions and want to do things to make them suffer or make desperate attempts to get back with them. All those burning urges like wanting to meet them, to understand why they can't meet you after you were both once so spontaneous and shared such intimacy? Why? Why can't they at least give you clarity? Did something you said or did influence them? What will you achieve by going through this, over and over again? The mad, impulsive ideas racing through your head are not such good ones.

The voice within you is trying to make itself heard. It is begging you to *let it rest. Do nothing.*

Acceptance is the only way to navigate impermanence in life.

We have no choice but to train ourselves to pause, to stop having knee-jerk reactions. Otherwise, all we'll do is damage ourselves and our health, mental and physical. If it's a given that everyone's life will have challenges, and your hopes getting dashed was a life challenge you couldn't escape, then at least stop resisting it. *Mitti daal, yaar.* (Put it to rest.) Stop wasting the precious little energy you have left on unproductive thoughts of revenge, stalking, or hoping they are miserable without you. Press the pause button.

According to every philosophy, when faced with loss especially, you have to value stillness. You have to accept change. Learn from the experience and transform. You're thinking, 'Yeah, they can talk. They are gurus. They don't understand my feelings. I feel '*jaise bikhar gaya hoon*' (strewn around).' But as I see it, *aur koi chara nahin hai*; we don't have an option in this. We have to put ourselves together, every scattered part, bit by bit.

Embrace the inescapable. Grow through what you go through.

Pema Chödrön, American-born Tibetan Buddhist nun and writer, advises we look at pain as a portal that we have to pass through to transform, and look at it as an opportunity for growth. I know it sounds airy-fairy, given how you're feeling right now. But for one minute, consider this: What if you could view yourself as a work in progress and allow for the possibility that this brokenness you're feeling is not how it ends? What if it leads you to a more beautiful version of yourself? The way a piece mended by kintsugi, the Japanese art where broken pottery is rejoined with gold, makes the piece even more exquisite and unique. Let the thought stay with you. I'm not asking you to accept it right away.

In fact, I do a hard eye-roll myself if someone tells me, 'Nothing is truly resolved until its lesson is absorbed.' I promptly want to text whoever is sending these tough surprise tests my way: 'Dear Creator: You know that test you keep giving me that I keep failing miserably? A humble request. I respectfully beg that you give me an 'F' and allow me to move to the next one. Thanks.'

Maybe we need to think of ourselves as an 'Alice in Wonderland', falling down the rabbit hole, imagining it as our pain portal, where this post-break-up period will actually transform us. I'm sending out another text. 'Dear Creator: While I'm in transformation mode, I humbly beg you, this time let me emerge with Ex-ray vision? To save future heartache.'

Love does not mean holding. Love is not a possession.

The nature of love is that it can't be owned. It doesn't belong to you or to any of us. It just flows through us. It visits us; it changes us. But love is not ours to claim for the length of time *we want.* It is a guest. Sometimes love is a long-staying guest. A beautiful companion who joined us for a significant part of our life. Even so, it will inevitably leave. It has to carry on in its journey. We may miss that guest for a long time. But they had their reasons to leave. And we have our reality to live with. And sometimes love is a guest who turns our life upside down. Their visit feels like a swift tornado passed through our life. One way or another, our reality is that the love that visited us has gone now.

As was famously said after every Elvis Presley performance: 'Elvis has left the building.' Love has left the heart it lived in briefly. It is gone. It is not coming back.

In any case – love is not something to be held. It is something to be lived.

All we can do is cherish the good parts of what we had, and that at least for some time we had it. Not everyone has that. We can only honour it and release it.

No coincidences: Andy's story

My life has been full of the craziest coincidences. I'm Armenian, born and lived in Calcutta with my family until I was about 18. Then I lost my parents and moved to Australia. Some years later, I'm a cop there. Young guy, missing a sense of home, living in my first home, outside Canberra. This old lady pays a neighbourly visit. Soon, she says, 'Hey, your accent has a lot of Aussie in it and a bit of Indian.' I was stumped; told her I grew up in Calcutta, India. She kept going, 'Where?' When I tell her, she's stunned. Turned out she and her husband had been my parents' closest friends. What are the odds, eh?

A lot of these coincidences happen to me. I've always believed there's a reason a person has been sent into my life. It is up to us to recognize their messages for us if we can listen and learn. Back then, I didn't. I married a woman called Diana on a massive impulse when I was 19. On the night of our marriage, I realised it was a bad idea. I had basically fallen more in love with the idea of her mum. Not in a creepy way, no. Just the warmth of her home, their curry-leaf tree, it was all reminiscent of the family I lost in Calcutta. Anyway, three children later and my being an absentee dad a lot, our marriage was over. And guess the name of the woman I was involved with right after Diana. It was Deanna! Crazy, isn't it? You can't make those kinds of coincidences happen if you try.

After Diana and Deanna, I moved to Melbourne.

One night someone called the station about damage to a property. So, I turned up there and met Jillian, the woman who made the call. I got busy, gathering information. At the end of it she said, 'I'll buy you a drink?' I said, 'No, no, that's not allowed.' She said 'oops' pretty cutely. 'Dinner's fine,' I quickly added.

A couple of days later we were smooching, etc. She was beautiful, her hair flying all over the place. We get to her place. And I can't function! Yeah, my boy chooses this time to get moody! And she's being all understanding, like 'It happens.' But ohh man. I was into her like crazy. Next time we were to go out together, I was practising snake charmer stuff to get the guy inside to make me proud. Again, we're together and it doesn't perform! I told my partner down at the station and he says, 'Mate, there's a solution for that!' I'm thinking he's going to say Viagra, and the fucker says, 'I can do it!' 'Right,' I tell him. 'I don't need teamwork on this.'

Finally, the third time Jill and I are together, she says 'Is it me?' and I think, no, it was my self-esteem, especially after my bad marriage. With Jillian, so stunning and confident, I felt a lot of pressure. Anyway, third time wasn't just lucky, it was brilliant. My boy did me proud and soon we were a 'thing'. Jill moved in with me and we got into all the couple kind of stuff, good and bad. Like, I've always loved playing the sax, it's a big stress buster for me. I look forward to my days off to play at parties. Jill wouldn't bother to come to my gigs. But hey, she sang in a choir and there I was, always at her performances; they were painful to sit through. These things aren't a big deal if the rest of it is solid.

One of the things that I wasn't willing to bend on was her wanting to have a baby. I mean I already had three with Diana. I wasn't interested in more. I'd been open about it from early on. In my heart, I was bothered that I wasn't even a good dad to my three. Luckily, they'd grown up well with Diana and her mother. But with my job in a different city and five years living with Jillian, I constantly felt guilty about not being there for my kids. I wanted us to shift back to Canberra.

Cut to two years later. Jill had started saying 'Let me get to bed first, let me fall asleep first. You come later, 'cause you snore.' So, for quite a long time, I was in a long, sexless, cuddle-less relationship with the woman I had seen myself getting old with. She was shutting me out from her life too, with no discussion.

Some years later I had gone to court to testify in a case. I met this woman Melissa there. I ended up in a relationship with her because it had become so joyless and sexless with Jill. We still acted like a couple, at least in front of friends. Home was just not a place I wanted to be anymore. I told Melissa what the scene was with Jill. I felt quite shit. Everyone knew me as this honourable, good bloke. Heck, I've even received an important bravery award for my police work. But here I was, spending more and more time with another woman, streets away from my own home. The stress was killing.

Plus, I could never make sense of the coincidences in my life. Like why was it that every important person in my life was connected with someone in my past. For example, just before I married Diana, I discovered she had the same birthday as my mum. Then the second

Deanna had the same birthday as my daughter. Then Melissa goes and has the same birthday as Jillian. Easier to remember everyone's, right? Often, I would try and figure out what the significance could be. There had to be something, isn't it, or why on earth would I have met that person? And each time it played out like a similar kind of sad song.

Jill was always working late hours or going out with her friends. I was still looking to mend things with her. We had been together so long. I kept trying to get Jill to commit to moving to Canberra so I could play a bigger part in my kids' lives. She kept postponing it.

Once, I asked her to come with me to my mate's wedding rehearsal but she said she was meeting a girlfriend. The next day, another freaky coincidence, I bumped into this girlfriend. We stood chatting. I discovered she hadn't met Jill in days. I couldn't understand why? Why lie? She could have said she wanted to skip the dinner.

Another time I was at a conference but I wasn't feeling so good. I got home early. I find this guy in my pool. I ask Jill what the hell was going on. She gives me a long story about how the guy's a friend, his wife's having an affair and he just wanted to escape the arguments for a bit. I told the man to get the fuck out of my place.

I had already called it off with Mel. Luckily, that ended smoothly.

Another time, I had come away to Canberra to see my kids. I wanted Jill and me to move there, make a fresh start. I even bought her ticket to come for a recce with me, meet the kids. Jill opted out, said she had work.

I'm heading back from my trip and Jill says she'll come get me from the airport. All the way home, she's being really nice, really charming. I couldn't believe it because I had left for Canberra feeling quite pissed off at her again not making any effort for me. I was not that keen to behave like nothing had happened, just because she came to pick me up. We reach home, she throws me on the bed; she's panting all over me, acting like she really wants me. I'm telling you I was not ready, no way, there was too much bitterness of the sexless years and now she is doing this aggressive grabbing me everywhere; she practically rapes me. I was shell-shocked.

A week later, a guy calls. He asks me, 'When are you moving out, mate?' He says he's in a relationship with Jill and she's told him I'm moving soon to Canberra. 'Should I come throw your stuff out?' he demands.

When Jill comes home, I ask if there's something she wants to tell me.

So listen to this. She says she met this guy when I was in Canberra, at some beach barbeque, they just took a walk, next thing he forced himself on her. So, I say to her, come down with me to the station. I'll get the boys to arrest him for rape. She backs off and pulls a big number on me. She tells me she's pregnant with our kid. That's when the penny dropped for me. She must have got pregnant with this bonehead and still wanted to feel more secure hanging on to me. Or God knows what.

But now I realised why she tried so madly to get sex to happen. I called the fucker up to get all the details I could. He even cockily described our bed. It's an unusual kind of bed. I asked her again, 'You sure he forced himself on you on the beach? How does he know our house?' She still kept blabbing and denying it. I'm thinking he's definitely seen our bed up close. Probably even fucked her on it. The bed I wasn't even able to cuddle with her on for years. For fuck's sake, I'm a cop! And this woman tried to stick me with another man's child.

Part of me was very conflicted because here was a woman I cared for. I have been on good terms with all the women I've been with, even my ex, even Melissa, who had been lovely and I felt quite bad that I couldn't offer her more because I still loved Jill. She was my Jill, my beautiful Jill, and I know she had been in love with me too. But then she put me through so much grief, those cold, sexless years, with no effort to be a partner to me at all.

Yeah, I didn't like this new Andy that came out of all this. Back then I felt like a victim, wronged, and played for a fool. Of course, I didn't like my double standards, that I'd also been cheating for a while with Mel. But it was that twisted part, of Jill trying to palm off another man's child on me that I felt most betrayed about. I felt good actually that I didn't get involved in her baby drama. It hurt a lot that my Jill could do this. It wasn't just that she stopped loving me. She wanted to keep using me. She even changed the ticket I bought for her for Canberra, to go on holiday with that baby-maker boyfriend! Do you know – coincidence of coincidences, his name is Andrew. Yet another Andy. He didn't even hang around long enough to see her through with the baby. I refused to get involved too. Told her to go get it taken care of by herself.

I was so bitter. I may even have cried on my partner down at the station. I took close to a year off from work actually, saw a mental health professional and understood that this psych stuff is good. In that year, I'd have this parade of pictures flashing through my head. I tell you – the trauma of my police work, seeing hacked-up bodies, the aftermath of a bombing or massive fire had not broken me up as bad as the breaking of this relationship did. That time, I had all the emotions going on, reliving the loneliness and humiliation, especially Jill trying to trick me into believing it was my baby. I listened to all the miserable love songs. I wanted to throw myself out of the window. I did it, but I was on the ground floor, so it made no difference, lol.

So where am I many years later? It wasn't as if I got sorted in an instant. I met two more women, both called Annie. I'm not making it up. One was a very short thing. I met the other Annie some months after it ended with the first one, at a friend's barbeque. I was looking for someone to catch a movie and laugh with. The spark wasn't great for me, but for her it was. It lasted a year but then it started to irritate the hell out of me. I just wasn't attracted and she was closed about trying things I love, like Indian food. We decided to go back to being friends and that's actually better, because I'm trying to be transparent too.

Finally, I looked critically at all these coincidences, these patterns, these loops within loops of the women I've been with. I'm teaching myself to stop looking for bloody connections in everything and face up to the kind of man I had been.

At least the current version of me isn't playing victim any more. In hindsight, I was a bastard. As a mature person, I can process it. Yes, I got dumped but I was equally responsible. Jillian had a yearning to be a mother and I had been rigid in closing the door on that because I'd had my three. A good partner would have put their arm around her and not been so mean.

This roller-coaster ride forced me to confront some uncomfortable truths about myself.

I hope I've learned whatever I was supposed to and someday, maybe, I'll meet a woman whose name or birthdate have nothing in common with anyone I know. I'm disconnecting the dots.

Out of words: Jonathan's story

You asked me about heartbreak. I've had three. Let's call them the three chapters in my life.

The first chapter was when my marriage of seventeen years ended. Helene and I met when she was eighteen and I was twenty-eight. We are both Germans and got married only when she was pregnant, as is the tradition in Germany. We had three children together. I love to be a father. After many years, we suddenly hit a stage where there was no emotional connection in the marriage. She was drifting away. I thought, is this even normal? My parents had been married till death, but Helene was always in a bad mood. After a year of long periods of icy silence, she suddenly said she wants to leave me. It was a shock but I didn't want marriage to feel like anyone is a prisoner in it. After we separated, I would see my kids on the street. They would wave to me and I had tears in my eyes. I would be fine to lose a relationship but not my children. They are a part of me. This was twenty-five years ago. It's not real anymore; the only thing that is real are my children.

Then chapter two, Linda. I met her through my sister, who set it up as an actual date. We were to meet at a café close to my studio. I teach modern dance, it's not as if it makes me millions; far from it, but I love it. Linda arrived at my studio before the café appointment. The first coffee date was so smooth. Words and sparks flew fast. She started dropping by my class often. We would get a meal after it, talking about our lives. Soon, we went on a combined holiday and fell in love. I felt rescued again. I felt good about the five children that came as part and parcel of her. It did make it more difficult to get used to each other with all the other tension factors but I don't like to blame or give up easily. I don't say yes to everything, I do like to protect myself. According to both my sisters, even when I was a young boy, I was influenced by nice movies or books, I was always looking for love. With women, not men. I've never been inclined that way.

Linda and I did a lot of holidays with the church. But quite soon a lot of arguments would erupt and it would always be about her kids, who were very rude. They disliked me. I could not tell them not to watch TV. It was always blaring. My children, who used to drop in to see me regularly, started to distance from her children. I was really feeling torn about all the conflict because I loved her and I love my children. We tried getting distance between us and meeting on weekends. I really looked forward to it. Unfortunately, once the crack had come, all that seemed to be escaping was a lot of angry words. On our last weekend, we talked and talked, for four or five hours. I was totally down. I could not have any ideas to help the situation. I didn't know what to do even if I was wrong. I convinced her to come to partner counselling with me but after one session she refused. How could I forget the beautiful beginning years that we had together?

But even for me, the hurt had started to pile up a

lot. If I'm in a relationship, I don't like to look around. I'm faithful. But in the period when I was with Linda, I lost my father. It was a very difficult time for me; my family has always been close. I was in pain, but she was looking at soccer and laughing; she felt nothing. What I was going through meant nothing to her. Some days later, maybe in a week or two, she said to me she met another man. I said, 'Go, go, go.' I was lost. I started to smoke a lot.

In the first relationship, with Helene, it had disintegrated slowly. The love had gone out over time, bit by bit. Once I met her crossing the street. We just said hello. So many precious years had been wiped out. It felt like I was running into a stranger. With Linda, even though it lasted only two years, almost all of it was about quarrels. I still felt love but I could not find a way to her. She was out of love even if she didn't use those words and now, we were just fighting with words. Words words words words words words words words words words all the time. I ran out of words.

We are still in touch. She's a friend; she still does my taxes for me.

With Linda, I knew she was meeting this guy at the sports bar. I felt hurt but as I said I was all out of words and still in love. My daughter also said to me, 'Yes daddy, you are alone now. But you've been alone a long time.'

You tell me how that helps when your heart is constantly hurting, constantly raw, and still hoping for something to change. I was fifty-five when I lost Linda. I was full of self-pity. My parents were together till the end. That had always been my model of love and a good relationship. After Linda, for four or five years, I was on my own.

What did help was that I still had a lot of love to give, and I kept giving it to my dance classes, my students, and more and more to my love for music. I met musicians, I played guitar. I played in a band, but I didn't even know how to meet other women. I think I didn't send signals because I was destroyed by the last heartbreak.

Then I met Lamai. I met her at a café. She's a Thai woman, with the prettiest, softest face and most caring personality. On our very first date together, I thought it was an awakening for me. I had felt I was too old, that my life had ended. I was glad that it was not a German woman because I didn't know if I could trust another one for the third time. Lamai was open, smiling – it was a cure for my heart. I went to Poland with her. It was like being drowned and then finding a reason not to drown. That emptiness and that constant sense of being alone that had been eating at me for four years lifted. With my two sisters and many women friends, they listen, they talk different. With them I could even talk about my dreams. I could never understand why it used to be different with the women I was in a relationship with. With Lamai, I felt like a withered plant coming back to life.

Lamai was married. Yet she did everything with me – walking, talking, looking for flowers, planting. We only had two quarrels in three years. In Manheim, she was always taking care of me. Lamai said it would be nice if I came to Thailand. I was honoured to see this side to her, to be included in her life. I went with her to Asia and met her family – her father, her brother. I had never gone to another continent. Her father had been paralysed for more than ten years. We took holidays on other islands also, I felt so relaxed. I was also doing music and that interest had been growing a lot. I finally started feeling as if life had had a purpose and my meeting Lamai was at the centre of it. It didn't matter to me that she was married. She barely ever talked about this absentee husband. One of my musician friends was having problems with his girlfriend and to be honest, I was feeling so smug and sorry for him. I'd never felt more secure in a relationship and in my life.

Then after her 50th birthday, she suddenly starts saying it's too far for her to come and see me in Manheim. The train is too far, that it gets too tiring. Within two weeks, she starts saying she has problems sleeping at my place. At this time, I was actively helping her to get divorced and had been putting my own money into it. I had even been helping her with her father's treatment in Thailand. Next thing I know she's found herself a room in Heidelberg in the centre of the city and suddenly she has moved out. It was like an atomic bomb for me. I began begging her, please don't destroy this happiness. How could it be that a few days before that she was holding my hand and saying I love you, Jon? And now I think maybe she was saying it and all the time she had been planning to leave me.

It was over faster than I could make any sense of what was happening. It was catastrophic for me. I bumped into her once in Heidelberg. I was a wreck. Just to see her broke me up. Once again, I was out of words.

I learned later that she went away to Switzerland.

I have no desire to know how or why. It would be too painful.

I agree I have no answer. There is no other man in her life now, that's all I know. I was thinking this time around, with this woman, my Lamai, it would last forever. The only reason I was interested in her culture was because of her. Because I was interested in her. And then I think I wasted three years. Three years. I would be lying if I said it was easy to pick myself up from the third heartbreak, the most catastrophic. I think maybe it would be like someone saying 'you have cancer.' Maybe that would have been easier for me to come back from than this. I tried to be strong for my sisters and my daughter too, who was pregnant around this time. I managed to hold back my tears in front of them. I did not want them to be in pain because I was.

I would love to believe in love but it's always hard to start anew. At sixty-five, I don't know if I have the capacity to do it again.

With every month though, I start to get better. I am still open to human beings. I love my music, I love smiles. I started taking more of my dance classes outside, by the river, and though it means it's less convenient for students to come there, to dance on the grass, to flow with the music, like the trees and water swaying with the breeze, it has somehow been talking to me, nudging me to not give up on life.

I would like to love again with all my heart. I like life. I'm thankful I am healthy, thankful for the beauty of nature. It gives me strength.

I have strong days; I have weak days. I do know now

that if you want to love, you have to be careful. Somebody like me always loves to give but I have to guard myself to wait for the other person to give some things back. If ever there will be another person, even if I was to have the same experience at the end of another relationship, I would not like to lose that opportunity. I don't want to become the kind of person who gets so closed that I let my past experiences destroy any future relationship.

My sisters say I talk much less now. I think of these heartbreaks and of each of the women at the centre of these three chapters. I think to myself: I loved you, I feel sad, but I don't want to stay angry. I feel lonely in the night; I feel lonely in the day. I have no one to say 'have a nice weekend' or to plan my day with. I know slowly time and nature will heal me. What's the guarantee you won't get hurt even when you're protecting yourself and feeling safe?

I live my life. Out of words maybe, for now, maybe for more years to come, but not all out of hope.

10

It's called a detox because it was toxic for you

∞

I'm not suggesting the ex was totally toxic. Maybe they were charming sometimes, especially in the beginning. Then they started acting differently with you, differently with different people, different at different times. Why should you waste your headspace on all that now? When their interest disappeared, when you look back and realise it had become toxic for you – that is it. That's why you need a proper detox. I'm sure you've had enough friends telling you to cut this ex out. To fire-wall their access to you.

Remember *Jab We Met* and Geet's advice to Aditya to burn his ex's photo and flush it down the loo? It was pure gold as advice goes. But today you need to work through your phone and purge their presence from your life. Maybe you even deleted some stuff, it lasted a day or a few, then you caved in again, restoring those pics back into the gallery, and plunged right back into that circle of revisiting your memories.

An emotional wound is like any physical wound. It needs time to heal. It simply cannot if you keep picking at the scab and opening up the wound that's still raw inside. No one but you can know how lonely it feels, and gut-wrenching to accept that it is over. I'm saying this with compassion and anger on your behalf. I need you to snap out of that sadness. If they had cared enough about you, when they knew you were hurting so much, and still behaved the way they did, they showed you their true feelings. *How dare you allow their hollow words to sit with you all hours of the day?! When they couldn't even show up for you in real life!*

No one is coming to save you. You have to be your own saviour.

The detox from the ex has to be hundred per cent. *Not to give them* any more importance, but *to give yourself* the importance you need.

I'll share something personal in the hope it helps you take baby steps to begin reclaiming yourself. One of my life's ongoing struggles has been with weight and my relationship with my body. In my early teens, I dreamt of owning a pair of Levi's jeans. I'd shared my measurements with an NRI aunt who was coming from firang-land and had agreed to get them. This was before we poor backward desis had heard of standard UK/US sizes. The aunt dumped the jeans on the bed with a ridiculing comment about my size. In hindsight when I look back at that size, I realise I was a pretty decent, curvy shape. But I didn't know any better. I had been fat-shamed. Yet again. It didn't help that my brother was skinny. Fat shaming still passed for humour in most North Indian families. Insensitive, ever-helpful relatives would make jokes like 'Stop eating up all the food. Leave some for your brother also.' No one told them off or told me I looked just fine; those were not the days of '*Papa ki pari*' (Papa's little princess) as they later became. Cut to years later. My weight had piled on during pregnancy and I was still working on rolling it back after having the baby. After months of struggle, I was thrilled I'd knocked off eight kilos. When I shared this achievement with my now extended family, all supremely genetically-lean people, it was received with disbelief. I was told how astonishing it was that the weight loss didn't show at all. That, *on anyone else, an eight-kilo loss would have made them look like the walking dead.* At the time, it really felt crushing. My motivation to keep trying to roll back the surplus weight had hit rock bottom with that verbal punch. I so wanted to not let it get to me. In fact, my WhatsApp status forever has been '*Hara wahi jo lada nahin.*' ('Defeated is the one who didn't fight.')

So, in that blazing summer, I feebly resolved I would keep trying to get back into shape. I decided I'd aim to get out for a walk post breastfeeding the baby and tackling home-related morning chores and before leaving for work. Mornings have just never been my thang. I was pooh-poohed. 'A morning walk at 9 a.m.? Since when is 9 a.m. "morning"?' Of course, it's easier to see now that I could have let it wash over me like water off a duck's back. But I was a different person, in a different world, and around 25 years old then.

The nudge can come from anyone or anywhere. Take it and run with it.

One morning an aunt, one of the gentlest people I have known, called just when I was debating my lofty plan of a 9 a.m. morning walk in the June heat of Delhi. I mentioned this to her. Some people might have encouraged you to relax, to forget it. This aunt didn't. She nudged me in a calm, encouraging way. '*Chale jao,*' she said in her soft voice. 'Just walk a bit. It's not so hot yet. There's plenty of shade on one side of the road.' (It was probably around 38°C outside.) Here's the best part. She made me feel I could do it, by simply suggesting small, achievable targets. 'Do it for ten minutes, *hai na, beta?* Ten minutes will fly; listen to some music or look around. Such nice trees in our area. Do ten minutes, then turn back. And you'll finish a twenty-minute walk comfortably.' She made it feel unpressured. I had a small, doable target of dragging my depressed feet for ten minutes, going down the road, then heading back for the same amount of time. I felt like just mayyyybe I could do it. I managed it, despite the scorching sun on my skin. My flushed face felt like a reward, for not letting myself quit.

What this wise, kind aunt probably factored in was that *momentum builds from small targets.* I kept increasing the time I would walk, going further down the road before turning back to the house. Soon, a ten-minute one-way walk became fifteen and I was walking fifteen minutes up the road, fifteen back. Without any pressure or negative self-talk.

If you're wondering what this has to do with you and your heartbreak, first promise yourself (and me, please) that from here on you prioritize yourself.

Your self-esteem has to be stronger than your feelings.

Prioritising yourself means recognising that what you need to break is an addiction. Being in love and all that comes with it is not that different from a drug addiction. The withdrawal is making you constantly text, call, go past their place, like their posts – these are like hits your body is craving when you are in withdrawal. Even if you were the one to end the relationship, seeing your ex with someone else can feel shitty, like you weren't good enough, that's why it didn't work. Us humans, we're silly and often insecure, we love to compare. Social media is largely built on envy. (It's my view, I'm not going to apologise for it.) Stalking your ex, squeezing info about them out of common friends, even creating fake profiles to check who they're seeing is all guaranteed to trigger. You can end up obsessing, comparing your ex's new partner with yourself, finding yourself lacking – basically multiplying negative thoughts. You cannot come out of this feeling better in any way! To heal from the break-up, you need to shut those triggers out. The only way to do it is to totally disconnect from their energy.

If it costs you your peace, it's too expensive.

Remember, how when we were kids our parents told us to close our eyes when there was a scary scene in a film. We do the same thing. It is instinctive to protect people we love from avoidable pain. It's just as important to protect yourself, your inner child, who is traumatised by the constant see-saw of emotions you're putting yourself through. That non-stop exhaustion of living with 'loves me, loves-me-not', and begging for someone's love, has to stop now. Think of Juhi, in the story 'Chemical locha', and the pain she put herself through after Rajat went off to Mumbai, pleading with him to give the relationship another chance. For him to turn around and say, 'Hey, we were just getting to know each other.' *Can anyone put a price on the time and the confidence she lost?*

If this break-up has got you in such a vice-like grip, recognise that it is an addiction. No two ways about it. You *have to* beat it. How? You have to see what this relationship actually cost you.

The price you have paid and are paying is in your own suffering. It is in the self-confidence you lost. It is all these weeks, months, maybe years of productivity that you've lost. And let's not forget what it has actually cost you in terms of a chance to meet other people. Your time, your good years, your peace! The cost of staying stuck is not just time you lost which you can reclaim later. No, it is gone forever. And the sooner you get strict about no-contact with the ex, the sooner you can walk free.

The 30-day no-contact detox from the ex, digital and in real time, is possible.

Yes, really. To get over any heartbreak, 30 days of completely cutting off contact are crucial. That's the bare minimum time you need to break the cycle of dependence and build emotional and physical distance from the ex.

If you didn't do it right when the break-up happened and have been stuck in a pendulum-like situation of no-contact, some-contact, no replies, killing silences, you're damaging your own self-worth. Even if you caved in to trying to rekindle it yesterday, forget it. Yesterday is gone. No-contact begins now. It is critical you commit to doing it immediately. Maintaining contact, even casual texts, just keeps alive false hopes of a reconciliation. It's cruel to do that to yourself. *How can you expect to get comfort from the person who is the source of your pain*? How? '*Tu dard bhi, dua bhi tu, zakhm bhi, dawa bhi.*' Wah, wah! It's brilliant as a song to play on a drive by yourself while you're still letting it all out. But do you really think the *marz*, the illness of lovesickness and addiction to the ex, and the *zakhm*, the wound that the bloody jerk, the ex, left you with, can be your remedy? Let's get real. I mean this seriously and with utmost compassion – your heart needs space to get clarity, to learn to manage your emotions.

Why should you do it? Because you didn't deserve this suffering. Why 30 days? It's what experts agree is needed to break a habit. Why go cold turkey? Because anything else is a cop-out. Unless you're in one of two or three situations where you are co-parenting etc., going cold turkey is the only effective way to try and break an addiction.

Commit to 30 days of 'no contact'. No compromises.

The thirty days of no-contact allows you to process the emotions churning inside you, grieve what you had and lost. By breaking the dependency, it forces you to find other ways to feel alive. *No contact for the bare minimum of 30 days.* No compromises. No negotiation. It is the boundary you have to set and stick to after a break-up. We're going to get there together, with baby steps.

Exorcising the ex

EXIT THE HEARTBREAK
EX-ray

The only way to release what isn't serving you is by understanding what you can change. You can't change the situation. You can change how you're letting it control you. For that, first, let's exorcise that ex.

What: Your assignment today is to see him/her through the eyes of the one or two critical friends you have.

Why: Today I want you to see that ex as the useless person they showed themselves to be. I am not here to be fair to your ex. I'm sure they have their own story about why it went the way it did. I'm not interested in it. My goal is you. To help you get past this emotional minefield you're stuck in.

How: List the most appropriate adjectives or phrases that ever came to your mind, about *that person who you undeservedly put on a pedestal.* Yes, that same @#$ who unceremoniously moved on, leaving you in this sad state. Write them all down. Be unsparing. Ruthless. Every quality or trait about them that your friends reminded you about. Examples: Bald, broke, stale breathed, entitled, double-faced, freeloader, wife-cheater, loser, mama's precious boy, can't hold down a job, user, gold-digger, spineless, pig, slob, petty, chipped-nail-polish-wearing, drama queen...you get the drift. Now write down, in marker pen on a piece of paper (or use your phone), a note as I explain below. I don't even want that person's name on it. Just do as I explain below.

'What ON EARTH am I doing, crying over a – – (fill in any words and details from the list you just made; more examples for you: Jowly, self-absorbed, lazy, stinky, nylon-shirt-wearing, cheap-fragrance-using, pompous, delusional, obsessed with their receding hairline, skin care routine, selfie-insane, wimp) loser of a man/woman like him/her who can't even – – (add what you want, this note is for you, and this is not the time or place to be politically correct! More examples: Can't even get it up without a bloody pill, can't even pick up a bill, can't even get along with her bestie, can't even fight for me, for us, can't even be honest with himself, can't even look after a bloody plant, etc.) Fat chance he/she was ever going to look after us! WHAT A RELIEF TO BE FREE!'

P.S.: Keep this note where you can reach for it anytime you feel low.

Power games: Vani's story

Aditya and I were dating for two years. My parents were open-minded and never questioned us. I had been open with my family from the time I met Aditya and even told them when it started getting serious. I was aware that our backgrounds were very different and I didn't want anything to become a problem later. His family had always been into politics. My father was a librarian in a college university; my mother worked with a government bank. Dad valued love. We were middle class. Yet, I got the best of schooling. My parents never held me back on what to aim for in life.

I had always imagined myself as a PR professional. That's how I met Aditya, at a press conference of the political party his family were part of. Sparks flew immediately between us. As a bright, young account executive, I would often be sent to oversee some press conference or other as this political party was one of our company's important clients. After a few such meetings, Aditya asked me to meet him in his office. I was impressed that he had this huge room, classy desk, people waiting for time with him while I could waltz in anytime. We got closer when I realised he was also fond of reading like me. I suggested we start a philosophy appreciation group. Vivekananda was a common thread we had. I was always reading him a lot. We knew a group of intellectuals between us, the young who's who of the city. I had organised a Creative Arts' Society too, invited famous authors and included Aditya too in it; he knew a lot of people in the art scene.

We became closer but still only as friends. My friend Supriya and I used to go out for parties. Around then, Aditya started chasing me. Those days I was attracted to the intellect. I wasn't able to gauge if they were good human beings. In fact, Dad was looking for matches of middle-class boys with good prospects for me. I insisted on having my way and marrying Aditya. My father dissuaded me about him, he said he didn't get a good vibe and recognised a feudal mindset.

Early into the marriage, I realised Aditya had massive baggage. His family were all powerful names in local politics with a lot of money and no daughters in the family. Although Aditya was Westernised and went to mixed parties, at no time before we got married – did I have an inkling that he came from such regressive thinking. All the time we dated, I only wore Western clothes. I assumed he fell in love with me the way I was, including my way of dressing. The moment we got married, it was expected I would only wear saris and fit into traditional bahu expectations. It became traumatic. Of course I was going to protest. In his view, 'the protest has to be silenced.'

So, the violence started. Sharp and sudden. It could be over anything, over food, over talking on the phone, really just anything. And then he was into womanising. I had studied at a convent school. I grew up believing what the nuns taught us, 'Do good and good will happen.' It astonished me that his family all had awful relationships with each other. Surprisingly, I managed to keep good relationships with them individually. My father-in-law's temper was well known, he could completely fly into a rage with anyone, without the least provocation. Aditya used to get jealous if his own father talked a lot to me. And there I was, innocently thinking I was building my relationships within the family. This had been ingrained in me. Aditya would get triggered even if I had an innocent discussion with my father-in-law on a general topic, or listened to him go on about politics.

Aditya read every single thing as sexual provocation, and always held me to blame.

Amidst the violence, confusion, womanising and that soul-deadening burden of keeping up a facade with the outside world, including with my friend Supriya, somehow I managed to keep my kid a little protected from all this. The house was huge. I made sure she stayed out of sight in one section of the house. Aditya liked that. I started seeing no chance of him changing. For three generations, this feudal, patriarchal, intolerant attitude had been accepted in their family. Like, there would always be this chair which was the 'man's chair'. No one else could sit on it. It was quite a task to keep my child out of range all the time, as invisible as possible. I used to do ordinary things with her outside the house, within the regulations of how long I could stay away. It became a little easier once Aditya won the local seat and grew in power. I escaped more often on trips with my daughter and turned a blind eye to him, as long as he didn't attack me. And by blind eye, I meant literally. He openly started bringing other women home and flaunting them around the house. I would pretend not to see it. It was the only way to cope.

Somewhere in all this, I started going for pottery classes at a studio nearby. When I started working with clay, something started changing in me. The physical act of surrendering control to the wet clay taught me to let go of the need for perfection. My marriage was far from it. All my bottled-up emotions, I put into shaping clay. It is not easy to describe, but it started changing me from a meek person to a person whose long-suppressed anxiety about consequences had started to shake off. By then the daughter had grown up, she was now stable. I started feeling a little freer. The world had also started becoming more open to women regarding divorce, alimony, and all that. I could never tell my parents about the problems in the marriage. Not when they had supported me in marrying into this family, despite my father's reservations. I thought, 'No way can I give my father this grief.'

You won't even believe all the kind of things that I used to live in fear of. Like 'photo *kaise tangi hai*,' (why is the photo hung like that?) or '*chai aise kyun bani hai?*' (why is the tea made like this?) How do girls even today allow themselves to become second fiddle? How did I continue so long in that dead-inside state, with someone who could keep hurting me. In my heart I used to think he must love me, except that something's got warped in his mind. I couldn't accept that he didn't care. I was still the mother of our child. The more he grew as a politician, the more he seemed to think it was ok for him to do as he pleased. His scathing comments, about my clothes especially, haunt me till today. Even walking around with the hurt, I would try to ensure his professional growth. What kind of conditioning gets so stuck in our heads at a very early stage? Maybe because I had seen my parents' good marriage, seen my mother supporting my father, I thought it was my duty as a wife. But I forgot that it is a two-way street. My parents always stood by each other.

I suppressed any questions in my mind, in the faint hope that things would get better. It took me a long time to realize I had stopped loving him many years ago. After my girl had grown up, I realised I was still tiptoeing around Aditya; always unhappy. My daughter would keep pressing the divorce decision on me.

It was finally the pottery that changed me. It made me more centred, and when you work with clay, you have to be able to think on your feet, solve a problem calmly. I became stronger internally, till I found the courage to move out. He sent emissaries to convince me not to divorce. With the kind of political clout he had by then, it was scary to think of how to face him. He started sending threats, like I could forget about getting anything at all out of the divorce, and that he'd shut down anything I tried to do.

I realised nothing mattered. Not the big house he had or the land. I used to cry a lot and especially when I used to practice pottery. Body-racking sobs, or sometimes I would laugh too much, uncontrollably, in odd situations. That time I couldn't understand it, but now I realize how pottery became meditative for me.

It became clear step by step. Earlier I used to feel

'death is better than divorce.'

I dreaded what kind of lies he would create; what kind of slander he would spread, just to cover up his own shameful behaviour. I was surprised at the strength I had within me, as the divorce started unfolding. Around that time, I also started a small business.

I used to pray to God at one time, 'Let me have his love.'

While the divorce was dragging out, I would keep praying to God again and again. But my prayer had changed to 'Let me at least experience love.' I must say God did give me that. And divorce and a decent alimony too.

I'm crying because I feel my pottery changed me. The tactile sensation of the cool, wet clay moving under your hands forces you to be completely present in the moment, quieting other thoughts. For me, everything that you're seeking can be glimpsed in the connection we make inside, as we make pottery. That's the part that's real. It also gave me a new identity as I went from being a pottery student (which never ends) to becoming a master potter and teacher. I built my reputation and I'm building back my financial independence slowly.

I feel my prayers were being answered most importantly in the way I started to make peace with myself.

For the last two years I've been involved with Srinivas, a man who is much younger than me. Like, much! This relationship was the answer to my prayers to God to 'let me at least experience love.' The relationship with Srini, my partner, started happening only when I learned this about myself. For now, I am enjoying feeling loved, feeling desired, feeling like a woman. (Giggle) Initially I had reservations about how my girl would accept this much younger man in my life. But I've been open with her. It hasn't been easy. I know she only wants to protect me; her intent is good. But I'm much older now. Being with Srini has been good for me, including learning how to handle my daughter's reactions and protect my happiness.

I cannot compromise any more for anyone.

11

The 3-3-3 plan to get you through no-contact

Remember I told you how my weight-loss goal felt so daunting but it became do-able when my aunt made the mountain feel smaller. I learned then that the trick is in setting small targets, achieving small victories, and building on that. Baby steps. That's what we're going to take together, from today.

The 3-3-3 no-contact plan: 3 day blocks, 3 rules, 3 rewards.

Part 1: To get through 1 day at a time, for 3 days.

Forget that this is about 30 days. That feels tough. All you need to remember is: small goal, to get through this day, just these 24 hours, with no-contact. Then you move on to the next day and then the next. Eye on the goal. Today. Next day. And the next. Done. That's how you will achieve getting through a block of 3 days. That's it. Block 1 done. One day at a time. And, gently, like that, you'll get through one more block. Then another block. Till ten blocks are done. At the end of this chapter, you will see an exercise called 'The 30 day no-contact countdown'. Please follow the absolutely simple instructions there to begin your 30 day countdown. Put up your 30-day no-contact countdown next to your personal manifesto.

This 30 days of going no-contact is an important step in breaking the addiction to the ex. Don't worry ahead. Only focus on honestly and successfully making it through another day and night. Easy does it.

Part 2: The 3 rules to get you through No-Contact.

Rule 1: Pack it, burn it, delete it, block it: a complete cleanse.

If there are keepsakes that stir up mixed memories, why do you even want them? Burn the damn things. It'll feel cathartic and empowering. Delete things like joint social media accounts (as in Yash's story of 'Controlled chaos'). It doesn't matter how many followers it had. You can't go down that road again. It'll feel tragic, but liberating too. If there are pictures with good memories, remove them from your phone. Back them up somewhere. Tell yourself they're there. Someday when you are stronger you may look at them. But not now. Intimate pictures, chat history, all your shared media do the detox. No exceptions. Ask your closest friend to be there, support you, let you grieve, but their non-negotiable task is to make sure it's done. As for the ex's phone number, all their IDs, email, social media, block, block, block. I mean it. Don't just delete. So that there's no way you can reconnect and self-sabotage. Remember you're doing this for yourself. Yes, it will break you again, but *you survived the worst part, the break-up. Now it's about your survival.* You don't need the thousands of texts, as proof that it happened. It was real. Now, your reality demands that you move on.

Rule 2: Pick and enlist a friend to be your tough-love buddy through this.

Hopefully you have some close friends who know about your relationship. Think hard and pick the friend who is not a softie at heart; who will not indulge you in your miserable lows, because let's accept it, the lows will come. The withdrawal from the person you are addicted to will hit you. That's when you need a tough-love friend who is capable of talking you out of any weak, lonely or drunk decisions. Who won't melt when you start off on how much you love her/ him, or that you think they are really sorry this time. In de-addiction programmes, they tell you - do not keep the liquor or drugs or the dealer's number where you can find it. (That's why the digital detox part.) Secondly, you should be able to call this tough-love buddy when you feel your resolve getting weak. Make sure you have a long, hard chat with this buddy before you start the 3-3-3 Plan. Promise them this time you really mean it; that they can pull out whatever tough love they need to stop you from going back to square one.

Rule 3: No exceptions in the 30 days of no-contact

I'm onto you. You're already thinking of ifs and buts to postpone starting. Like 'I'll start next month. I'll wish them on their birthday/Diwali/Christmas at least.' Or, 'I'll send them a gift for that special day. What if they try to contact me then and can't reach me because I blocked their number everywhere. That'll be a tragedy. I won't even come to know if they tried contacting me.

Maybe they'll text that they miss me. No, I can't block them.' These are all panicked excuses you're making because you're trying not to close the door on it.

Tell yourself right at the start, and your tough-love buddy too, this will happen. Anticipate the crash, as addicts often do. You know it'll come. Your mind will try to convince you why it's essential you find their number again and send just that one random message as a way to remind them you exist. Anticipate that you'll feel that insane craving and make yourself (and your tough-love buddy) so damn proud that you controlled your urge to connect. One day at a time, you promised yourself, your buddy and me.

And if somehow the ex reaches out to you, promising to change this time around, even then, please, I beg of you, *do not compromise* right now. You can explain in one to-the-point text that you're not ready to have this conversation right now and to respect that. Remember, it is your call now. You have to draw the boundaries. Don't act like a beggar for the crumbs coming your way.

The no-contact plan doesn't mean you you'll get over the person in 30 days. It means you gave yourself the essential space to get over the addiction. Once you get past that mind-numbing, obsessed state of yearning, you can evaluate what comes next, from a calmer place.

To overcome any difficult situation, your inner dialogue is most important.

If you tell yourself stuff like 'their voice makes me so weak, I become mush when they say they miss me, I want to see them just once more' - you know you've lost the battle already. Train yourself to hear your toughest teacher or boss' voice to straighten yourself out and stop any defeating thoughts.

In my worst moments, and there have been many awful ones, when I have wanted to drop with fatigue and despair, I have one overriding thought which is 'You've got through worse, Milan. You'll get through this.' When I've been running around hospitals as often I have, with my husband's long battle with an incurable auto-immune illness, sitting with him in ambulances for the nth time, I dully have these words going through my head, 'I've got through worse. I'll get through this.' I may allow myself a flash memory of what the previous worst time of my life was, how dark it looked. It's a brief reminder to myself that I may have thought it was impossible to survive *that.* Questioned whether there was any God, or anyone in the world to whom I matter? But I do know I made it through that time, and I have to remember I can get through this too. I have to remind myself each time, I am not a quitter. I am my father's daughter.

I'm sharing these extremely personal moments of doubt and how I talk myself through them so that you check your self-talk too, to get through each difficult day, one day at a time. Tell yourself whatever motivates you. Things like, 'I do not accept that pathetic apology. I deserve better. I'm not accepting crumbs any more. I won't settle for less.' Or 'I got through those entrance exams, didn't I, when everything that could go wrong went wrong. I'll get through this time too.'

Yeah, life sucks, sometimes. Is this a situation of your making? Is it in your control? Not entirely. All that is in your control is to manage yourself, get through the unfair, lousy, painful part. And get through it with your head held high.

Part 3: The 3 rewards of the 3-3-3 'no contact' plan

Reward 1: Physically ticking off one more hard-fought day on your 30-day countdown

I hope you've stuck your *30-day countdown* printout where you can see it and track your progress. It isn't just one small tick. You know that it took you one full day + one night further in staying strong. You fought the urge to give in, you told yourself firmly, 'I'm going to sit with that silence of no pings, no calls or anything connected to them. I'm bloody proud that I'm not acting on my impulse. I made it through another difficult few hours and I'm still holding strong.' Each small tick is taking you closer to achieving a 3-day block. Block by block, you'll do ten of those 3-day blocks. Believe me, you will start to look forward to giving yourself this triumphant tick mark every morning. It's a reward and motivation in itself.

Reward 2: The best revenge is living well. Not to show off. But to show up for yourself.

Make a 'Living well' list of at least 60 things you enjoy and haven't done much of, ever since you were involved with that ex. It's a fun exercise; these are things you owe yourself.

Done? Now, every morning after you've ticked off another day of no-contact with the ex, look at your 'Living well' list and pick what you'll do today. Remember this reward begins on Day 2 as your reward for ticking off Day 1. On Day 31, you pick something from the list for ticking off Day 30. Your ideas don't have to be expensive. Jot down a mix of some indulgences and some that are bigger on experience. Be sure not to lose perspective on why you're doing this. It's a daily achievement reward to yourself, with something that lets you live in the moment. Enjoy that. But don't get addicted to something else in these 30 days, while trying to break out of the love addiction. For example, trying out a new cuisine. One day, ok. Daily, no. *No new addiction needed, got it?* That's why your 'Living well' list has to be thought through. My personal favourite is trying to learn salsa. I am the world's best worst dancer and even my supremely kind salsa instructor agrees. He refuses to promote me to level 2 but the salsa sure lifts me out of low moods. And so I return to every other salsa beginner's batch as their most enthusiastic, uncoordinated, undefeated student.

Ticking off things from this list is not to show off or make anyone jealous. It is to *show up for yourself* by living well every day.

My favourite poet Mary Oliver asks, 'Tell me, what is it you plan to do with your one wild and precious life?'

Reward 3: You did it. Damn, you deserve to celebrate this biggie, your Independence Day.

Ultimately, the biggest reward for getting through each day, each block, and getting to the finish line of 30 days 'no contact' is breaking free of the debilitating feeling of being tied to your ex. You are free. You did it. This is your Independence Day. Now you can go forward with well-deserved self-respect. Wonder of wonders, you can feel yourself healing, even if it's not in a glory hallelujah way.

What's the third reward, you ask. Well, a friend of mine landed up in town recently after her long, contentious divorce came through. We agreed that it called for a celebratory party. At the very least, I'd suggest you have a happy Independence Day celebration with your tough-love buddy. Include all others, the friends and family who have held your hand and held you back from every bad impulsive decision in this meaningful celebration. Once again, the celebration is to mark something significant that you have achieved. It needn't be fancy or expensive. Just find a good way to mark this day and also to say thank you to them and yourself.

You deserve to give yourself a special pat on the back once you've completed the 3-3-3 no-contact plan. Plan ahead during the 30 days for something that'll be meaningful for you. Maybe tickets to a major concert you've been dreaming of going to, a big sporting event, or trying an adventure sport you've dreamed of (with a clean health chit from a doctor of course). These 30 days of no-contact will also have helped clear your head to the extent of letting other dreams surface. Like maybe becoming a screenplay writer or lyricist or life coach, or learning an instrument you loved. Dream big, why not? Use this milestone, your first Independence Day from the person who broke your heart. Sign up for something that lets you follow your heart (not in a romantic way, but with something that was a childhood dream).

Navigating post-break-up contact when 'no contact' isn't an option

I understand the 'no contact' rule can't work for everyone. If you're co-parenting, you need to communicate about your children. Ignoring your ex in that situation is likely to become problematic. Similarly, if you share a mutual friend group (let's say you fell in love because of a common love for performing music and the friend worlds continue to overlap) or a common interest group (maybe you are part of a project that still needs to be completed, a film needs to hit the floors, careers and people's reputations and money are at stake). In these types of situations, completely avoiding your ex might be impossible. All the more critical then, to establish and maintain *clear boundaries.* Limit communication to what is *strictly necessary,* keep conversations brief and keep emotional baggage out of them. Yes, you have to navigate your shared responsibilities and overlapping social circles. But your bigger priority has to be you. Your goal is to *minimize contact* as much as possible and create distance from your ex. The 3-3-3 plan of getting through 3 days at a time, with 3 rules and 3 rewards is still for you, except that instead of 'no contact', make it *'no contact beyond absolutely necessary'.*

Deal?

The 30-day 'no-contact' countdown

EXIT THE HEARTBREAK *EXcellent*

Step 1: Select a calendar

It can be any physical or digital calendar to track the next 30 days. Better still, print out a calendar page.

Step 2: Colour code every 3 days in a different colour.

Step 3: Mark the countdown Write the number 30 on the date you begin, 29 on day 2, 28 on day 3 and so on, till you've got number 1 on the last day. In the next date, write in capital letters: FREE

Don't wait till next week, a Monday or a 1st. It's not important. Begin now. Look forward 30 days from now, to the day you can be free of your addiction to the ex.

The goal: Just get through today (24 hours) with no contact. And then the next and next. Focus only on making it through this day. Remind yourself of all the bigger things you've achieved in your life.

The reward: That triumphant tick each day. Nights are tricky, so tick it off only the next morning, for the day and night you completed.

3-Day blocks: One day at a time builds into a 3-day block. One day at a time, one block at a time, 10 of these blocks and you've made it. You'll get through this!

Your 'living well' list

EXIT THE HEARTBREAK
EXplore

Someone wise said, 'Living well is the best revenge.' Think of it this way. It's like killing two birds with one stone. One, you live out all the interesting things that you had put on hold because your ex's interests didn't match with yours. Two, you get to have the last laugh, because instead of breaking you, the break-up actually becomes the reason for you to grow. Give free rein to your imagination. Haters gonna hate. You're gonna amp up the fun, baby!

Rules: Your 'Living well' list should have at least 60 ideas that involve your a) getting out of the house; b) getting into an activity that brings you into contact with other people; and c) getting out of your comfort zone. (This automatically excludes activities that take you down roads that are connected with the ex. For example, if hiking was your shared passion, for now keep that out of your list. There is nothing to be gained from doing anything triggering.)

Be sure to make a list of 60, so that in the coming 30 days, you have plenty of options on what you'll do as your reward for the day. I'm throwing out a few ideas here, like signing up for a walking tour in your city, or taking a short cooking class (I did one in Thailand; I may not remember a thing I learnt to cook there, but it was worth every baht I spent, just to meet 10 new people from different countries, laugh together and eat some great food at the end of it). Or you could go back to building good health. It could mean joining a new fitness activity, a self-defence class – whatever you feel drawn to.

Remember that song 'Living la vida loca'? It means 'Living the crazy life'. And who's to say what crazy means. One person's leftovers is another person's crazy curry! You're the cook. Cook up your crazy 'Living well' life.

Hugs for free: Arun's story

∞

I was seventeen when it all started. She was my best friend's girlfriend. She, as in Sharmishta. My best friend, as in Dinesh.

One day, Dinesh said, 'You go and speak to her. I want you to break us apart.' He wanted to end things with her without doing it himself because 'she's getting too intense.' He wanted to avoid a showdown. I was an introvert. She was my junior. I went to her directly and told her.

Our first interaction was on a college trip. Sharmishta and I started talking, I got to know she was crazy about Dinesh. He was my best friend but he was really cringy, the way he used to objectify women. And yet he could get a woman to become his girlfriend so easily. Sharmishta was no different, blind to it. She agreed to whatever he said. She couldn't see he was simply toxic. We would talk a lot, twelve-hour talkathons through the day and night. I saw Dinesh getting jealous. I felt ambivalent. I didn't want to get between them. Still, she was the first girl I spoke a lot to.

We had a challenge: whoever called first had to buy breakfast. It started feeling very couply. Often, I'd go with them like a third wheel. I was aware of it, even apologised to Dinesh. I'd say, 'You carry on.' She would protest vehemently. Yet she would often ask me to drop her home. I started to think maybe she's not sure herself who she wants.

One day she called me and said she had split up with Dinesh. I felt so good, she chose me over Dinesh. The next day Dinesh also told me they had split up. I felt so special. I felt that even if she hadn't said it, she had seen through Dinesh's fakeness and chosen me. Me. Arun. Arun Kuri. Not Cryri Arun as they tormented me in school. In school, kids used to tease me, hit me and plunge me in water. If I spoke to a girl, they would make a face, I couldn't understand why. If I told my dad I don't want to go to school, my dad would also hit me and say '*Kyun nahin jaana?*' (Why don't you want to go?) That made me cry.

Now I felt everything had changed. I was the one Sharmishta chose. She called me every day, came home often. Her mom also trusted me. Once Sharmishta went to Thailand, she got me a T-shirt and watch. I felt she really cared for me.

On my birthday, at midnight she didn't call. I thought she forgot. Next morning I saw 29 calls and 59 messages from her. That's when I knew my feelings were strong. But she got gifts for Dinesh also and asked me to give them to him. The next day I saw her sit behind him on his bike. It was strange. I thought maybe she wants to talk with him. I went and saw a movie on my own. I wanted to know what happened. She kept cutting my calls.

In my first relationship in high school too, Dinesh had come in between. Still, I never broke off our friendship. I knew he wanted a free bike ride from me but I was in awe. He was everything I wasn't.

I couldn't understand what happened with Sharmishta.

Even at eleven at night, we used to drive to the outskirts of Mysore, to the hills. We had some intimacy also on those rides. I felt elated she felt safe with me, she was opening up to me. Then after two days of my going on calling her, I got a message. 'It's over. I can't speak with you.' I texted her, 'Why did you do this? Did Dinesh say anything? Your family?' She only replied with an 'OK'. For the next two days I was walking around like a dead person. I felt like a stone. I felt acute pain. I just couldn't handle it.

I used to be an average student but this year I had been obsessed with her. I flunked. Then Dinesh casually confirmed they were back together. I texted her, 'You said he's toxic and now you're back with him?' She replied with some nonsense. She used the word 'love'. That hurt. It came as a big blow. I said, 'I want to throw the watch outside your house.' She said, 'Why? I gave it with love.' Love! I thought of the way she had used that word so differently for him and for me.

Looking back, I can see I was like a junkie, constantly in need of a hit, even a shitty text reply, and the pain it gave me was better than no contact. I believed that was all that I was worth.

One day Dinesh logged into his Facebook from my phone and didn't log out. I saw his texts to her telling her not to text me. I read every single message between them from April 23rd to May 9th, the exact dates she stopped talking to me. He even told her about what I had told him long ago in a weak moment, the school nickname I hated: Cryri Arun.

I realised it wasn't love; it was betrayal. For three

weeks I didn't leave my home. I let people think my depression was because of failing the 12th. Six months later, I still couldn't detach from her. Then in 2017 I came to Bangalore, cleared my 12th, joined hotel management college. My friends pushed me to text her again. We spoke briefly. I felt annoyed at how it had changed.

One day, I took her out for ice-cream. Later I texted her: 'I think I'm in love with you.'

She blocked me. The weird thing was after telling her, I went through everything in my head. I realised I didn't love her; I was addicted to her. I felt so liberated. I didn't have any urge or pain. I felt oddly happy saying 'I love you' to her, even though it led to this unhappy ending.

I started working at a 5-star hotel but soon developed anxiety and panic attacks. I even had suicidal thoughts. I got to know that there were bets on who would drop out of college first and it was all bets on me. In 2019, I had the worst panic attack. I couldn't breathe. I couldn't trust anyone.

Last year another girl who I thought liked me – we used to speak hours every day – got back with her boyfriend and stopped speaking to me. It felt like the Sharmishta experience all over again. I realised my trauma was unhealed. There's a voice in the corner of my head telling me I'm not ready to trust anyone. Words like 'you're not alone' felt empty and washed over me. My confidence in myself had become garbage.

I asked God for hope. I decided on a date to take my own life. One day a guy asked, 'Are you OK?' I broke down. He promised to take me to therapy after the pandemic. That's how, in 2020, I started therapy. It reopened a lot of the deep hurts. I could, slowly, sometimes share what I felt. How my sad relationships had damaged me.

Even my friends started opening up with me. I don't know when the idea came to me, to help others who were in a bad mental space – what I had only now started to come out of. I had seen videos of people in the US, holding big placards with messages like 'If you are going through depression or anxiety, hug me.' Or, 'You deserve to be loved for who you really are.' 'Feeling sad? Can't talk to anyone? I can give you a hug.'

I decided to do the same.

Before starting this, I thought if I can help even a single person, I'll be happy. My idea is only to create awareness about depression. People may not be willing to share their whole story but may tell me a little. I'll try to always be genuine, show my empathy and offer a real human connection. That was what I had felt so much in need of in my worst low time.

In January 2022, I started standing on Church Street, Bangalore, and in Kolkata too. There were people who laughed in my face. On the first day I did this, holding the boards, I thought people were judging me, looking at me like 'What's with him?' I ran away after a short time.

Sometimes things turn out in a way we can never imagine. I might never have found the courage to go back and stand on Bangalore's most happening street with my 'I can give you a hug' boards. But then something happened to make me stop thinking about myself and do what my heart had been pushing me to do.

My cousin took her life. That became the decisive moment for me.

I was shaken that she had never found anyone to talk to. I realised I too had been so close to becoming so locked in my own dark sadness. And for what? Some girls and friends who I now saw as hollow people. Their lives were carrying on. After that I was so sure that I don't care what people think.

Every weekend I stand on the street holding my boards for four, five hours. Meditation also helps me. I do it daily. Now I first ask myself if something gives me peace of mind. I trust a little better, especially myself. I stay away from people who feel toxic. Just today two guys stopped to talk to me, one hugged me and told me about his depression. His friend was zapped. He didn't know that his own friend was going through so much. He asked his friend, 'How come you didn't tell me?' This has happened several times in the last six months. Some newspapers have also interviewed me. Maybe what I'm doing arouses their curiosity. It's not important to me. For me, this is about a commitment I have made. If sometimes people stare or giggle, that's fine. There are those who come up, hug, sometimes they talk, sometimes not much, sometimes for very long.

I continue giving my hugs for free.

The bigger picture: Vijay's story

∞

I was twenty-two when I got involved with Bela, my first girlfriend. Till then I hadn't talked to any girl. I came from a conservative, business family in Kerala. It was expected that I would take over our business of selling coconut coir gift items. I was the only one in the family who had travelled outside our district for a deal.

I met Bela on the train. Much later I realised how low the odds of us meeting were. It was Bela's first time on a train in Kerala; her family had spent many years in Muscat and just returned to their native place. She started talking to me while waiting for the toilet to get free. I was brushing at the sink outside but of course I offered to let her use it first. I brought her chai at the next station. We spent the rest of the trip constantly talking and drinking endless chai. Every cup we ever drank together after that took us back to that first meeting. She proposed to me to be her boyfriend.

At that time, I was blind to everything, except being near her. This was my understanding of love. It was an all-consuming need for her. I was very possessive, as if I literally had the first right to her time and interests. Even if she went for a movie with her brother, I felt that she could have gone with me. Or if she joined a gym, I wanted her to join mine. So, imagine when she told me she got into an MBA programme in Hyderabad, I straightaway said 'no, you cannot go.' By then we were in love, but not lovers. Our parents had got involved; we had exchanged rings. When I said that to her, she asked me to meet her the next day at a restaurant. She went on in English and even French, which she spoke fluently because of her Muscat years. I didn't understand a word. Then she threw the ring on the plate and left with these final words: 'You were born in Palakkad, and you'll die here. You're not going anywhere.' That really hurt. I had gone to the restaurant to say to her, 'Of course, go to Hyderabad. I'll also get a job there and join a professional course.'

The next day I told my close friend Benoy, 'I've left my dad and the family business.' I actually had. It wasn't pleasant. I got a job in Pune to get far away from her and them, to start from scratch.

It was the loneliest time of my life. In Pune, I stayed with a friend, then moved to a place outside the city. I had a lot of time to myself. I felt free too. After years of dating Bela, I was liberated from the constant 'maintenance' work – no mails or messages to say I miss you, I love you. It's not as if I was forcing myself to do it but it meant a regular commitment to constantly reinforce the love.

Till then I had only heard Malayali music in my life. This became a time when I started listening to other music. I also started reading more. Bela had told me not to call. But within days of coming to Pune, I felt miserable without the anchor of the relationship. I gathered the courage to call her.

She went ballistic again. I felt like a worm.

I met a few people after that who wanted a

relationship, but I had withdrawn. It didn't feel right to jump into something else. I immersed myself into getting professionally qualified. I used all the headspace that had got freed up in studying astrophysics on my own. It had always fascinated me.

I met Bela again many years later, quite accidentally. I was working in HITEC city in Hyderabad at that time. I was standing near the fountain, smoking. At the other side of the fountain, I thought I saw her. I called out. She came running and hugged me. It felt like the easiest thing to sink into her hug. By then I had married Jahnavi. An impulsive marriage, to a North Indian woman, with a lot of resistance from both families. By then, the honeymoon phase was over and I had begun to see a suffocating, compulsive obsessive side to my wife.

Bela told me she had also married but it hadn't gone well. Her husband's mother was very controlling and even dictated when they should sleep together. Within a week they had divorced. Bela had changed a lot, from intense to bubbly.

Talk of bad timing. My wife was expecting when I met Bela again. As often happens when a marriage is already strained, pregnancy and hormone changes added to the fireworks. I couldn't see myself leaving my wife, not at such a time, even though Bela was single and still into me. Not that she said so but why else would she start coming to my office once a week, an hour's drive each way. Meeting her became one of the few things I looked forward to, as home started to feel like hell.

Bela and I never talked about anything romantic after the break-up. It was just there, unsaid. I had been through too much sadness, missing her, feeling rejected, to not have learned that one person cannot become your life. Those four years had taught me to focus on and build my career.

I still had butterflies in my stomach when I saw Bela in 2004. But that inner conflict remained. I had fought so hard to reach that shift in my emotions; to feel free. Even within my bad marriage, I was no longer a prisoner to my emotions as I had been before.

I let it roll. Every Friday, Bela would come to my office, we'd go for a drink, then I'd drop her home, have food; I even slept over a few times. With nothing else happening. I still had high regard for her. She will always have a soft corner in my heart. Having sex was never the endgame.

We stayed friends. For me, there was no question of leaving my wife, with a child in the picture. Over the years I travelled a lot. Later, when I went to the US on a project, I got a mail from Bela – she'd met a guy on a marriage portal and married him. That too ended soon. We still had this in common, the habit of acting in haste.

Talking of haste, during her second divorce I came to Palakkad to see my family. She was also visiting hers. I went to her place one day when no one else was home. Not for any other reason, except that Palakkad is small and meeting outside would lead to gossip. I was washing my hands at the sink, almost exactly like when we first met on the train, when Bela came up behind me and said she regretted breaking up with me. That is the only time we've had sex.

One important thing I credit to that first heartbreak,

was the drive it gave me to prove myself. Her remark that I'd never be anything but a small-town boy angered me and pushed me to move out of my comfort zone. I wanted to earn a six-figure salary on my own steam. Back then, there was no social media to show off on. I didn't even care to tell her. My goals had changed. In my mid-20s, I was changing jobs, making friends, meeting new women. Sex wasn't a big thing for me at that time. It was something I saw as part of marriage. Casual sex also happened, and it stayed casual.

The other important thing heartbreak did was screw up my confidence on a personal level. Once it happens, you think you'll fuck it up again.

When I met Roma around 2002, I was hesitant, underconfident and never able to tell her what I really felt. My inner dialogue was, 'She's beautiful but she won't like me.' I ended up losing a woman that I loved, and still love; but know there is no point in going down that road.

I'd always been curious, always living more in my head. In my bad marriage I had time to think about my patterns; how those two relationships could have ended differently.

The interest in astrophysics that had begun in Pune when I was rebuilding myself continued. It made me look at things outside myself, outside the planet. I used to look up random science-related stuff on YouTube, and teach myself about other planetary systems. It put my problems in perspective. 'Why do we give so much importance to a relationship?' I'd imagine myself out in space; a dot that couldn't even be seen in the darkness somewhere on the earth; silly me, crying silly tears over something that had no lasting value. I started feeling life was too big to get sucked into our small emotions. We human beings are so insignificant.

I speak to Bela twice a week, mostly about what's happening in her life. It feels good that we are connected, though I don't feel a need to see her. Not even for a movie. I know I will never sleep with her again.

When it ended badly with Roma, and I felt that same 'poor me', 'why me' sadness as with Bela, I reminded myself to 'look up!' Literally.

I look at Bela and Roma as people I grew up with; they're a part of my life. I don't associate them with pain any more.

I haven't seen Roma for over four years. Once, on her asking, I met her quickly near her office. She hadn't divorced then. Sadly, she hasn't moved on. She says her life revolves around me. She keeps texting, calling, silent phone calls, just our breaths and things unsaid. I haven't left WhatsApp groups we share, knowing she finds comfort in seeing me there. I thought, let her rebuild. I don't respond directly, knowing she will eventually see we cannot be together.

I wish I could tell her she needs outside intervention. I don't mean just deleting all the texts, but to look outside ourselves. To look at the bigger world and see how small we are.

12

What you do with your suffering is your act of resistance

∞

At one time, I decided to return to work full-time in advertising after a gap. I had moved with two young children to a city where I practically knew no one. I had got the designation that seemed important then and the money I asked for. It felt fantastic to be back writing ad campaigns, which I've always loved. The job soon turned out to be a bummer. I discovered I had next to no team. I couldn't hire, couldn't fire. It didn't matter that I put my all into it, won the agency a crazy amount of new business, at the cost of barely seeing my kids in that feverish desire to 'prove myself' again. I had slaved, prayed, struggled with next-to-no-sleep, and next-to-no-support. When that job ended, as it invariably had to, I was devastated. I was in a full-on victim state of mind. I resolved I'd be my own boss from then on.

I had no way of seeing ahead, to know how this was the best thing that could happen for me. Professionally, as a consultant, it worked out surprisingly well. No complaints.

More importantly, I had freed up some time for myself. I started writing short stories, with no client diktats, no deadlines, no plan to get published. On a lark,

I entered a short story for a contest by Harlequin UK. To my complete amazement, I won. It made me India's first Mills & Boon author and gave me a little more than my 15 minutes of fame. It brought me priceless experiences like hearing my story performed and broadcast on BBC and being interviewed on the iconic BBC Women's hour show along with Penny Jordan, the goddess of romance, by the legendary Jenni Murray, who has interviewed everyone from Queen (the band) to the Queen (the Crown).

Here's the thing: *there is no way I could have had the bandwidth to write the winning short story had I still been in that killing job; the one that I cried so much over losing.* I could never have seen in those failure-filled lonely days that life had a different, thrilling plan for me. That a whole new adventure lay ahead of me, as an author. And it would give me much wider scope to tell stories than I could have ever thought. So what I'd like to suggest is:

One: When lousy things happen, trust there's a bigger plan which will reveal itself.

Instead of getting stuck in the victim mindset, as I too had initially (and there will always be people who love to turn the knife in your wound), remind yourself there is a bigger plan for you in it. It doesn't matter if you can't see it right now. Just trust that *there is a reason* something didn't work out. The reason will reveal itself when the time is right for it. And when life has dealt you a load of lemons that leave your mouth with a sad, sour taste, please resolve, my friend, that you will start lemonading. You will take your unique heartbreak experience and add a metaphorical dash of vodka to your lemonade. Or you will create an art installation out of the squeezed-out lemon skins. Trust that your day will come. Your only job is to come unstuck first from the sticky lemons.

Two: Our goal is not to suffer passively. But to make something out of it.

We don't realise it but we make living in pain our comfort zone. Why should you waste your pain? This state of mind when your suffering is so intense and potent - is a hotbed of creativity. Pain fuels growth. Pain fuels creativity. Take your pain and make something out of it.

Murakami said, 'Pain is inevitable. Suffering is optional.' To which I'd like to add: Suffering is a passive act. Instead, channel it into action. Not the destructive 'I'll show him/her' kind. Not at all. For all that reactive thinking, the rule is still 'do nothing'.

The heartbreak pain will take its own time to process. After you've completed 30 days of no-contact, allow your emotional struggle to push you to find meaning. Try to do something with it. Find your own unique way to make art out of it. Make it in a way that helps others feel seen and heard. Who knows, it may make you a messiah for suffering souls.

Let me tell you about a heartbroken man whose ex's love for chai led him to start a 'Bewafa chai wala' stall.

In Patna, heartbroken people find their way to a tea stall called Bewafa chaiwala. Chhotu Gupta was 18 years when his sweetheart turned out to be *bewafa* (a promise breaker/unfaithful). His ex apparently had quite a passion for chai, so Chhotu decided to open a tea-stall as a way to remember her. With a twist. He offered his now-famous masala chai for just ten bucks for the jilted; for those whose love turned bewafa. For the rest, whose hearts are still intact, the chai costs 15 bucks or more. Chhotu says that almost 99 per cent of the people who gather around for his chai have been betrayed in love. Some talk about the *dhoka* (betrayal) and some don't. But as they gather around with others, there is comfort in feeling understood. Ask Chhotu if he thinks they actually have a broken heart or are doing a dhoka on him to get discounted tea, and he shakes his head, to indicate 'no, no'. Heartbreak is so common, he says. He hears them speak as he keeps turning out a thousand-plus cups of tea every day, well into midnight. How did I know of it? On an episode of *Kaun Banega Crorepati.* That's how an idea that comes from pure intentions connects and grows.

The point I make here is Chhotu didn't just stand at a stall drowning his own heartbreak sorrow in his ex-girlfriend's true love, chai. Life served him lemons and he lemonaded.

Like Kate Perry, Taylor Swift, Arianna Grande, let heartbreak help you find meaning.

There is so much raw pain when Kate Perry sings, 'We keep all our promises, be us against the world. In another life, I would make you stay. So I don't have to say, you were the one that got away.' Or when Adele sings, 'Hello from the other side, I must've called a thousand times.' Or when Taylor Swift sings 'Last kiss'. 'I'll watch your life in pictures like I used to watch you sleep.' So many artists have built their following by writing from the authentic place of their heartbreak. And let's not forget, a broken heart doesn't hurt less just because you're a pop superstar. If anything, it's probably even tougher to handle when you're in the public eye. Taylor Swift says, 'The only way that I can feel better about myself, pull myself out of that awful pain of losing someone, is writing songs about it to get some sort of clarity.' We see the hit albums. What we don't see is that it comes after personal struggle and a lot of work. I have to admire that she didn't just take creative inspiration from her epic breakups; she used them to evolve. From writing from a place of pain, to owning her story. Today she owns all the music she ever made, even the unreleased songs. That's defeating not just your inner demons, but also the capitalistic systems and patriarchy! Maybe soon she'll use her voice to fight bigger sorrows in the world. We can hope, can't we?

Selena Gomez, Katy Perry (after her divorce from Russell Brand), Rihanna, Ariana Grande – so many songs speak about power dynamics in relationships, how they've been treated by their partners and how they overcame it through self-confidence and resilience.

Gloria Gaynor's 'I will survive' was *the* survival anthem for women in the 80s. Now, Ariana Grande's 'Thank you, next' is it. She reflects today's attitude when she sings: 'Look what I got. Look at what you taught me. And for that, I say… Thank you, next (next). Thank you, next (next). Thank you, next. I'm so grateful for my ex.'

One day, my friend, you too will get to this point.

You think nothing could be as complicated as your sad love story? Listen to this.

Billy Joel (singer, songwriter, pianist) fell in love with his best friend and bandmate Jon Small's wife, Elizabeth Weber. How disastrous is that? To lose your best friend, and bandmate and then Elizabeth too walked away from him. It led to major depression, which eventually resulted in him writing songs that became his first big hits.

Heard of the complex love triangle between Amrita Pritam (writer, poet), Sahir Ludhianvi (lyricist, poet) and Imroz (artist and writer)? Amrita and Sahir loved each other deeply and passionately, though they never married. Amrita was willing to walk out of her unhappy marriage for Sahir but he wouldn't commit to their relationship. It ended when another woman entered Sahir's life. Amrita found solace with Imroz, who helped fill the void in her life. Sahir continued writing songs including about unfulfilled love, like '*Chalo ek baar phir se ajnabi ban jayein hum dono*' (about two lovers becoming strangers to each other).

Three broken-hearted people in a publicly known *love triangle where each one found creative outlets* for their emotional turmoil. The heartbreak must've been unimaginable, but how much richer the world is because of the work it led to.

Ideas become big when they come from powerful emotions and pure intentions.

Many artists quite literally turned their pain into art. Auguste Rodin's painting 'The kiss' is famous for its theme of unrequited love. Frieda Kahlo's legendary painting 'The two Friedas' represents two self-portraits: the Kahlo loved by Rivera and the Kahlo rejected by him. It comes out of her volatile relationship with her husband Diego Rivera, which swung between passionate highs and bitter lows; inspired by Rivera's insistent cheating (including with Kahlo's sister) and Kahlo's infidelity too.

Sofia Coppola (Francis Ford Coppola's daughter) wrote her film *Lost in Translation* based on her experience with her husband Spike Jonze. Apparently, Jonze had a mid-life crisis and cheated on Sofia with another guest at their hotel. The film's main character's husband gets up to similar shenanigans. A memorable film scripted from powerful emotions.

Or look at Deepika Padukone. After her highly publicised split from Ranbir Kapoor, the dignity with which she conducted herself, continued to build an impressive body of work, even worked on some projects later with her ex, shows so much resilience and growth. Most inspiring of all was how she committed to creating awareness about mental health. She has spoken on many platforms about how she initially felt a persistent emptiness, anxiety, and bouts of uncontrollable crying. Her mother recognised the symptoms of depression and got her to seek professional help. It led Deepika to create 'The Live Love Laugh Foundation' to raise awareness about mental health and provide support for it. A powerful example of pure intentions that led to empowering others after a heartbreak.

Truth and fiction. You only have to look around to find inspiration.

I'm giving you many different examples of ordinary people, celebrities, real life heroes and fictional characters to push you to make something out of your heartbreak. Think of it as a poke from life to channel your emotions and turn your life around.

Remember 'Legally Blonde' where the woman gets dumped by her boyfriend for being a bimbo. What does that do to her? It pushes her to get into Harvard Law School, become a successful lawyer and get the real revenge I wrote of earlier. Of living your best life!

If you're going to say, 'But that's not real life,' re-read the stories in this book. They're all inspiring and based on real life struggles. Look at Juhi in 'Chemical Locha' and how she has come such a long way, from being a battered wife with a special-needs child, to becoming a woman who helps other women in abusive relationships find safe refuge, and fights to repeal unjust laws. Or Vani, who came away from a long marriage to a powerful politician and narcissist. Her journey to becoming a master potter and claiming her happiness with a younger man is the stuff of films. Take Raminder/ Rama's story in 'Mirrors can lie'. We see Raminder come into embracing her identity as 'Rama', a trans woman. Not just that, Rama has become a voice for transgenders with a huge following on social media.

There's another powerful true story I read in 'Humans of Bombay' – about Neeta. Neeta had a physically abusive mother, an alcoholic father, was abandoned at the age of six, brought up by grandparents who married her off at fourteen to a man who became an alcoholic and was abusive. They had children, struggled financially, lived in a slum, but Neeta never gave up. She learned to drive scooters, cars and vans. Her husband would constantly gaslight her with words like, 'You can't do anything.' It only pushed her to try harder. When he threatened to kill her, Neeta knew she had to leave. At 34, she finally separated from him and prioritised completing her education along with her children's. During this time, her school bus business also started to do well. Parents felt safe letting their children ride in Neeta's vehicles. Today, Neeta owns 13 buses. Despite a series of shitty life events, Neeta didn't stay stuck in a victim mindset. She drives her decisions and business now and gets invited to talk with influencers on Instagram.

Heartbreak is the reason, but it doesn't have to be the central theme.

There are many shows and films about love, loss and the emotional tsunami of heartbreak. But they're also about so much more than that. Like *Sex Education, Heartstopper, Kal Ho Naa Ho.* My favourite is the Hindi film *Queen* in which Kangana Ranaut gets dumped on her wedding eve. To get over her heartbreak, she chooses to go off solo for her honeymoon. She ends up finding confidence, new friends, comes into her own, and has the adventure of a lifetime. That's so much better than being a morose Devdas type. The point I'm making is, yes, agreed, that *pyaar toh hona hi thha* (love was inevitable). Also agreed that suffering is part and parcel of love. But I disagree that you should let it consume you.

It sounds outrageous, I know. But allow yourself to feel a little gratitude for this experience. It is leading you towards the updated version of you. Where *you decide not to suffer passively.* You are taking the pain of heartbreak to *make something actively,* as a way to help you make sense; maybe even find purpose.

The act of creating is the important part. Not what it may or may not lead to.

I love what Prince, the legendary musician, says. 'The music is a success upon creation.' Meaning, the fact that you channelled yourself and your energy into creating something, *that is your success.* The rest is incidental.

What do you want to create? You'll know that by listening to what your mind is pushing you towards. Someone with an entrepreneurial spirit might channel their frustration into building a business that gives them a sense of purpose. (Like Neeta's school buses or Chhotu's Bewafa chai wala). If a bad relationship highlighted a need that wasn't being met, a person might develop a product or service to address that need. (As Deepika Padukone did in making support for mental health more accessible with The Live, Love, Laugh Foundation) A techie may turn their suffering into writing code for a dating app for broken-hearted people. Call it 'Burnt in love'*: Matches for those burnt in love. (*My idea. Don't forget my royalties if you decide to build it.)

At the very least, *look at creating a 2.0 version of you.* These words may sound like just words to you right now, but believe there is something better ahead for you. Like my example, like the people in this book, this experience is a catalyst for your growth.

Look at Vijay in 'The bigger picture'. It took Bela's rejection to make him break out of his comfort zone and build himself professionally. Look at Arun in 'Hugs for free' who came out of severe depression and overcame his social awkwardness to now help others with depression, by offering genuine hugs.

Don't waste your pain. Please channel it.

What's holding you back? Sometimes, people can't get a project off the ground because they worry about using from their life's experience, in whatever they plan to create. Especially about the sensitivities of other people involved. And rightly so. I have one suggestion to make. Create first, evaluate later. If you postpone putting your energy into this burning story that you want to tell, that energy will change. Your feelings and the story will change. First create whatever your heart is pushing you towards. Later, take a hard look at things like possible consequences, your comfort levels, checking legal liability, etc.

This story that is living inside you has an energy that is precious and unique. Don't let it slip away. Begin anywhere. *While you're creating, park the concerns.* Tell the story through whatever form is calling to you. It could be through making a unique piece of pottery, writing beautiful code, making a collage, outlining a new show. Maybe the traits of the ex will be useful in shaping a character!

At a session I was attending at Jaipur Lit Fest in 2013, someone asked Howard Jacobson (Man Booker-winning author) what he felt about using the truth from our lives in a story. Jacobson said (I'm paraphrasing) that there is no such thing as the truth. He used a relationship break-up as an example. There is the Dumper and the Dumpee (the one who got dumped). The Dumpee has their story. The Dumper has their story too. They are true and valid for both of them. Neither version is *the* truth. It's only 'their truth'. There are also versions of the story from the perspectives of the Dumper's friends and the Dumpee's friends, and of others not so closely connected to them. All those versions, together, may come somewhat close to the truth, he said.

So make something from this experience. At the very least it will help you make meaning out of it.

If it weren't for heartbreak, we wouldn't have so much beauty in songs, films, books, the unexpected wit pushing through a tearful moment in a show. *Imagine, you could also be creating something that will live.* Something that could be bigger than this shit show you've been stuck in.

Writing this book was my act of resistance, with the intent that I can reach you and everyone going through heartbreak, to say that we will come through this. And it will be as stronger people, changed for the better.

Moth to a flame: Sofia's story

∞

I'm Sofia Sanchez by birth but IMO it's just an accident that I was born in Mexico. For as long as I can remember, I was drawn to Hinduism, India, and especially Tamil culture and people who I found breathtaking. In 2017, I had gone on an app to learn about Tamil culture. I came across this Tamil guy Suresh Chandrasekaran, who was living in Florida. At that time, I was living in Tijuana, just South of California. We exchanged messages for four months. Soon I was calling him Chandru. I was about to graduate and had planned a trip to New York with my mum.

I'm an only child and there's nothing that my mother has not supported me in.

It was Christmas. Chandru and I agreed to meet at JFK. He was 27, I was 22. We met, gave each other presents. He was going back to Tampa. I invited him to visit me in Mexico. By New Year's, he sent a long message, that this is all that I want to do with you. I want to dance, go on a date with you, cook and eat Indian food with you, see you in an Indian silk sari, lie down with you and listen to classical Carnatic music, I want to show you all that I love about the place I come from, etc. This list itself was so magical that I think I had fallen in love with him already. I'll admit it wasn't the first time I was in love with someone, but this time felt different; predestined. We met in Orlando for a weekend, to turn that fantasy list into real. He got me gifts like stuff for Indian food, rented an Airbnb near Lake Tallahassee. One day for dinner I wore the beautiful shimmery sari he got for me. He helped me drape it. I felt alive and dying with the passion I felt for him. Can you believe it, he had never kissed anyone before me. He told me I was the love of his life. Also, that his sister had once fallen in love with a non-Tamilian, but their parents were not ok with it. So, there was no chance he could marry me, a non-Tamilian, and not-even-Indian girl.

The first time we had sex was beautiful; it was his first time. I showed him how. I've never held back my emotions. By the end of that weekend, he was crying about us parting. I was crying too, wishing I'd been born somewhere else. Chandru kept saying, 'You shouldn't wish that.' I was inconsolable. He said he's told his parents there's a beautiful, kind, Mexican girl he likes a lot. I thought maybe there's hope for us.

We kept meeting – for Valentine's Day, then for my birthday, then again in Vegas, another time in Austin. He kept saying we shouldn't meet; it would only prolong the inevitable. I kept insisting. He, in turn would insist on paying for my travel, etc. He was in software and was waiting for his visa renewal.

I got a job in Tijuana. I knew that once I began, I couldn't travel. I pressed him to meet me once more. I couldn't accept that he didn't realise what we had was really special. It led to our biggest argument. He said, 'If you love me, accept me as I am. I am a dutiful son first. I can't disillusion my parents by marrying someone they don't approve of. I cannot confront or leave my family.'

On the last day before we had to return, all we did was argue. What a colossal waste of that one precious day we had together. He took me to a jewellery shop and said, 'Pick a ring.' He said, 'You know that you're the true love of my life.' I knew the pressure he was under but my heart couldn't accept that he wasn't willing to fight for us. That was in August 2018. It got more complicated. I returned to Mexico and then he says his visa application was rejected, he has to go back to India. That he didn't tell me earlier because he didn't want to ruin our last trip together. Later, he said that his lawyer managed to get his visa renewed.

I kept asking him to come across to Mexico to meet my family, but he never did, saying he feels bad enough he can't marry me. He said he's decided he'll soon go back to India to meet girls that his parents would shortlist for him to see.

My friends tell me that was a load of bullshit. That he should have told me before our last trip about going back to marry the girl his parents picked. But it wasn't all lies. I know I was his first love, his first lover, and nobody can take that away from me.

We agreed to meet one last time in Orlando, to part on good terms. He told me the family pressure became unbearable; they had decided on a match for him. I was stunned he was going ahead with a match with a girl he'd never met in person, but he was. I was consumed with jealousy imagining the great South Indian beauty who would have my Chandru for life. A part of me kept hoping this would all vanish. After all, he was still meeting me every time I insisted. He was still saying I am his true love.

In 2020 I started working in a restaurant, but by end-March, with the pandemic starting, the restaurant shut down. Chandru was still in America. I knew I had to stop texting him, but he had got into my blood and all I wished for was I'd been born in a different skin. How differently our destinies would have played out then. We agreed to have one final phone call to give both of us closure. On that call he told me, 'Sofia, promise me you'll go after your dreams.'

Then he goes back and marries this ugly girl and produces a baby within a year and three months. You know what hurt the most even when I thought nothing could hurt me any more than I was already hurting? Looking at the live stream of my Chandru's wedding on YouTube. I watched it numbly. We had promised each other we'd tell each other about everything good. He sent me the link to the event.

I was like a moth drawn to a flame, bent on its own destruction. Watching him go around the fire, round and round, their hands tied together with sacred cloth, with this ugly woman. I wondered how he could have settled for something like that in his life. I wished I could flaunt myself in front of her. I wanted her to see me in my sexy bikini. I wanted her to discover that I was the one he had been dating, the one who had been his true love. I wanted *her* to go up in flames with jealousy. But of course, I didn't do all that. I only tortured myself with these thoughts.

I had several dreams in which someone said that I will have him in another life, in another skin that I'll be born in. I had all these questions, 'Why do we not get to choose?' I know he still loves me and he did not get to choose. Now we are in touch sporadically. I give him updates on what I'm doing. He won't say 'I love you'. But sometimes he'll say 'smart girl' or 'cute girl'.

Despite my sadness at not being born a Tamilian, I started being very grateful for the family that I'm born into. It's a family where no one tells me what to do or not to do. I'm still grateful I got to experience this kind of true love. I was often so angry, but Chandru never reacted. He would say, 'No, don't share this with your friends; they won't understand me or my culture.' This experience helped me develop a spiritual side to myself after I started to question these things. This thing of wishing I was born in a different culture – I think maybe I'll wish it hard enough for it to come true in my next life. There's definitely something out there with greater capacity than anything I can control. One day I did text him and asked him, 'You promised me, we made a soul contract to be together in another life.' He said if he has any say in what happens after this life ends, that contract stands.

This yearning took me years to quieten. Seeing Chandru's wedding changed me. I realize that it was meant to toughen me up. Earlier I was over-sensitive, a cry-baby. Now I just can't cry. It's been more than four years now since that day.

I had promised Chandru I'd go after my dreams. But later, he stopped being the reason for me to chase my dreams. As someone who has always believed in destiny, I know there is something beyond this love that I am meant to do in this life. I saved really sensibly working at the restaurant; enough for me to be able to pay for a master's degree in Berlin. I called to tell Chandru that.

Do I believe there's another love in store for me? Part of me feels, 'No, not really.' My mother, my grandma are both divorced. I've never felt them look for anything more, after their one big love. I know that you can be happy by yourself as well. I quite like the idea of being on my own. Seeing the livestream of Chandru's wedding changed me. I've become more private. These last four years, while I was saving money, holding on to my job and then going on to do my masters – no one had access to my private life except one friend and my therapist. I put my feelings into writing my poetry. My next dream is to get published.

February 13th, 14th or 15th?: Trixie's story

∞

We're sitting at this bar. It's packed. There's one seat empty at our table. Two hours in, this handsome guy, Greg, asks if he can sit next to me and Tina. Tina leans in and says, 'You should really get on with him, Trixie.' By the end of the night, he asks, 'Would you like to go out for dinner?' And I say 'yeah'. This was all new and interesting, in my early days in the UK. I knew right away that if Greg asked me out, I'd break up with Shaurya, my boyfriend back home in Toronto.

Greg asked me out on Feb. 13th. I asked Tina, 'Is it okay to break up with someone around Valentine's Day? What would be kinder? 13th Feb. would be cruel; I'm sure Shaurya would have organised flowers. Feb. 14th? No, that could scar him for life, I don't want to be that person. Feb. 15th looks bad too. Like you pretended to be a couple through V-Day and then bang, next day he's history.'

Let me roll back. My roommate at Uni in London, Tina, she's Asian-American, started dating an older guy, Phil. She wanted me to come out with a bunch of their friends. I had already started feeling iffy about Shaurya, my boyfriend, and friend since school in Toronto. When Shaurya and I started dating, I thought 'perfect, we're best friends, it can't be better.'

But soon after, he went to college in California and I went to London. Different time zones. All he wanted was to talk. Like, all the time. And I knew I have four years here. Shaurya and I broke up earlier too, then got back together in freshman year. Long-distance relationships are tough, and with time differences, even tougher. It barely lasted four months. I ended up kissing another guy, Greg. The one I met at the bar through Tina and Phil.

I emailed Jackie, my best friend in Toronto, about kissing Greg. This was pre-WhatsApp. Shaurya read it on her phone. I asked Jackie if she told him. She still says no. But how else did he read it? We were all such good friends, the Toronto gang. Now, everyone else is still friends but Shaurya and I are just acquaintances. That's one regret I have about dating a friend.

Shaurya's story was different. After I ended it, he was broken, put on weight. But now he's married to a brown girl.

I've always been a romantic though I don't come across that way. I was born in Toronto. Dad is Sindhi, raised in Mumbai. Mum is Gujju, grew up in Baroda. They ended up together in Toronto, running a successful family business.

My family weren't sold on Greg. We didn't let it get in the way. Greg was fun, four years older than me, and a little older than Ranjan, my brother. Ranjan felt like why is this tall, white, older guy from Liverpool chasing my sister? Why does he wear an earring? Studying film. Is that even a stable career? What is his scene? What's his intention? Just your regular Indian older brother.

It lasted four years with Greg, from 2009 to the end of 2012. Unsurprisingly, Phil and Tina didn't last. Phil has a thing for Asian girls. Later, Tina ditched me because I was still with Greg and he's still friends with Phil. (So messy, when friends turn to lovers, and if friends' friends also turn to lovers; one break-up and everything gets rocky because the circles still overlap.)

Greg's family had fully accepted me; I'd often visit them in Liverpool. Greg wanted to go see his pal Sammy in Switzerland before starting his internship. I had just landed an internship I'd really worked hard to get. No way I could join him. So Greg went off saying 'I love you, going miss you like mad.' But his buddy was busy with a new job. So Greg says to me, 'I'm getting bored, I'm going someplace warmer.' He was into biking. He decided on Palermo, Sicily. I'm saying to him, 'Go, get some sun, have fun,' while I threw myself into my internship.

We had set up a Skype date. He missed the date, then he says, 'I need to talk to you.' I had a horrible feeling. He says she met this girl and ended up going home with her. I asked him, 'Did you sleep with her?' He says 'no' very firmly. But then he says, 'I need to come see you, Trix.' By then it was almost Christmas. I was going back to Toronto. And that's my thing – family Christmas.

So I was thrilled when he says he want to come see me. I say, 'Wow, you never actually visited Toronto.' It would be the first time he'd meet my family. I asked Mom if he could stay at home. Mum agreed. Greg and I looked up fares, coordinating flights to land at about the same time. But I felt something was weird. Then suddenly he says the Palermo girl wants him to stay. I was furious at her and him. Her, for trying to steal my boyfriend. Him, for throwing everything away for her. In hindsight, I should only have been mad at him. I went to sleep that night, not knowing if he's going to Palermo.

I was young; even these questions should have been enough warning, A couple of days later, I'm flying London-Montreal-Toronto, a convoluted Christmas everything-is-overbooked route, carrying golf clubs for Dad.

Right before I am to board my flight, Greg calls, 'I don't think I can do this.' I said, 'You can't bail on me now.' He saying, 'I don't think I can put on this happy face in front of your folks.' When I get to Montreal, I pick up my iPad, connect and see his mail, 'I can't do this. I have to go back to Palermo.' I remember feeling like my stomach dropped through me to the floor. I wanted to throw my iPad across the airport lounge. It was crazy late at night too; I couldn't call my friends; everyone would be asleep.

I get on the plane. My brother's picking me up. I'm in Toronto, at the baggage carousel, only seeing a blur as the luggage belt moves. No idea how long I waited. No sign of the golf clubs I checked in.

My brother calls again, hear my voice, says, 'You okay?' I say, 'I'm waiting for the golf clubs. They seem to be lost.' He says 'Forget them. Come out.' He's heard my voice and he's asking again, 'Trix, are you hungry? What's wrong?' I finally walk away. I get in the car with my brother, and he says, 'Greg is coming later? You want me to come to the airport with you to get him? You must be tired.' Then I break down. Tell him Greg isn't coming. My brother takes over. He says, 'I'll speak to

Mum and Dad for you.' He did. They didn't bring it up the entire trip. At that time, I was presenting it like it was a mutual break-up. It was the worst Christmas.

We still emailed. Greg kept saying even a week later that he got freaked. He said, 'I know it was a big deal for you that your parents like me. I panicked a little.'

A year later he messaged me that I didn't deserve what he did. 'You were the best thing I had.' By then I was a little over it and I was getting updates from John, his roommate, that Greg was very upset. I can't lie. It felt good. That at least he mailed me. And he apologised.

I'd still bump into him because all our friends were common friends. Later, he kept wanting to come back. One day I returned from work and saw him waiting on the steps in the cold. I think he had genuinely been very confused. I was heartbroken. He had been my one true love. It was an all-consuming love. We used to spend every day together. I couldn't imagine my life or even London without him. I felt as if even the city had been completely ruined for me. And in January it can get so grey. So cold. I would keep crying on the Underground. I would have given anything to get back together with him, even now when so much had changed. I would still hope to run into him and pray he would be as broken as I felt and he would ask to get together again.

I would meet him at some common friend's place or birthday. Our worlds overlapped, there was no way I could completely cut off from him. He's saying he wants me back; I want him back too, but I have a feeling that Palermo girl is still in the picture. He would keep oscillating too, sometimes saying, 'I don't see it working between us.' I see it now, but not then.

Next year, Memorial Day barbecue. I'm with Tina. Good food, wine flowing, summer dresses. We see Greg's there too. Tina's angry on my behalf; even throws a drink at him. I had already decided to move back to Mumbai. We knew we're not going to meet again. We ended up sleeping together. It ended really nicely that way with us. Next morning, he gets a text message saying, 'Did you go to sleep alone or…?' He says to me, 'What the fuck. That's from the Palermo girl.'

One day, on a long video call, he says, 'I'm happy in Sicily.' I'm in bed with my laptop. My Facebook is open in another window. I see a hand with a ring. It shows up on my Facebook feed because she's tagged him in a picture; they are engaged. I literally got up and threw up, because just ten days before that he was sleeping with me. We were together four years. And this girl, who he barely knew for a year – he gets engaged to? He didn't invite any friends to the wedding. They speculated maybe it was for her visa, to get her to the UK, or maybe she got pregnant but that didn't happen. They've stayed married, have a kid too.

I moved to India soon after. It took me ten years to move forward. Now that I am where I am and I am with the person I'm with, you know? Kind of like that film '*Sliding doors*' about how mundane moments can change the course of a person's life.

I didn't see anyone for years. Initially in Mumbai, I got busy helping Dad with his business and then started my own. I was living with my brother. He's older, and well, Indian, which means he's very protective of me. I was always being introduced as Ranjan's little sister. It was fortunate actually. Because it gave me that space to get my head sorted out. Life kept life-ing.

After Greg, there was Param and Shrey. Both relationships ended up leaving me feeling like a lost case. Param really messed with me. I'd been straight from the start that I wanted a committed, leading-to-marriage relationship. And he was always like, I'm not ready to get married. A month later, he goes and gets married to someone else.

And Shrey. We'd been pretty good with each other, physically just brilliant, seeing each other a lot, keeping it light but still intentional. There was no one else we were involved with. I had my own start-up by then; he wasn't too invested in how that was going, but I figured we both had a lot going on. Juggling work and carving out time together can be demanding. One day, my parents were coming to Mumbai, I casually asked Shrey if he'd like to join us for dinner. He says, 'I don't know if I'm comfortable with that, if I'm ready for a relationship. We don't know where we are.' I'm thinking, 'You don't? What have we been doing all this time?' This 'I'm not ready for a relationship' thing started feeling like a recurring theme. A daily soap opera in the life of Trixie. The Shrey relationship left me really insecure and shaken. I would ask myself, how could I just not have had a read on this at all?

I started thinking about how most of us Indian girls tend to do 'future masturbation' – basically getting pleasure out of an imagined future. We'll be on date three with someone, think this person seems like a good catch, and already imagine getting married. I started thinking about how I had never been made a priority by any guy. We have to think about how the person makes you feel.

Gaurav and I first matched on a dating app. He had the most mediocre dating profile; very average photos, mundane info like 'he likes swimming'. I could see he seems tall. I had met a guy once who claimed he was 5'11" when he was actually 5'6". And I am 5'7". I was expecting anything. We matched then but didn't actually meet. Gaurav says he deleted that profile and uninstalled the app. A year later, I was 35, single, wanting to date, but after filtering out the crap. I matched with him again on a dating app. Now I decided to pay for the premium version and narrow my options to a smaller pool. For women, there's a lot of swiping, swiping, screening. I saw his profile. The same, no chest-thumping stuff like 'he likes swimming'. I remembered that. I always like to make the first move. I usually send the same thing to everybody – a gif of Kim Jong Un waving his fingers. It's funny because the responses you get from people can be so different, they tell you so much about the person. We realised we'd matched earlier but never met.

Interestingly, an astrologer once told my mum that I will have five great loves in my life. If I look back, there was Shaurya, then Greg, after Greg, Param, then the asshole Shrey. And finally Gaurav – my Season 5.

Now it starts to get more fun. I'd told this friend I was going on a new date. Caution, see? In case you get murdered, you want to be sure somebody knows where you are. Anyway, I was off to see Gaurav. This friend says,

'Gaurav?' She asks me the last name. Says she knows him and the family very well. His mum lives two homes away from hers. How had our paths never crossed? So many common friends, we've probably asked them, 'Know any single people you could set me up with?' None of them thought of introducing us!

Gaurav has strong female influences: two sisters, 7 and 12 years older than him. He's like literally the joy of the family. There's a difficult father-son relationship. The earlier version of him was a party guy. He did more drinking, was a smoker, did a bunch of drugs too earlier. And all those are a big turn-off for me, especially a smoker. If I'd met Gaurav earlier, I don't know if it would have worked out. Another interesting part where our lines crossed but we didn't meet. His ex, Neeti, went to the same Uni I did in London. He visited her there but we never saw each other. Gaurav and Neeti had been in an eight-year toxic relationship, and engaged twice. He had all that stuff to work through. I had to go through my four other relationships to get to Gaurav.

From the beginning Gaurav said that he really liked me. I was unsure because I was messed up in my head after Shrey. I still wasn't embracing the fact that Gaurav genuinely likes me. It took me a lot of time to get to understand what being secure feels like.

In January there's a music festival, Lollapalooza. Of all times to go sober, Gaurav chooses this very week to prep for a meditation course. And I was saying, why now? Sober dating is no fun! Early dating needs drinks to flow, after-dinner drinks, drinks to just hang out, etc. Anyway, I'm at Mahalakshmi, he's headed to pick up non-alcoholic drinks, I'm off to pick up sandwiches. I run into Dash, Ranjan's closest friend. Immediately he's texted him, 'Hey, your sister is seeing someone.' Ranjan is in town, says he needs to meet Gaurav. Up until then, a part of me still hadn't let go of Shrey. I wasn't seeing this other fun relationship I had with Gaurav. Then Gaurav and Ranjan meet and hit it off so well that Ranjan turns around and tells me, 'It'll be really awkward if you guys don't end up together.' And I say, 'No, no, Gaurav hasn't said anything yet about being exclusive.'

I told Gaurav about Shrey, about all my relationships, all the drama. Like, see me at my worst. I thought it would make him run away; it didn't. By contrast, with Gaurav, it was all calm. Even though he was going through a lot, with his dad and his toxic ex, the cards were all on the table. Gaurav was always transparent with me. It took me a while to realise that it didn't have to be dramatic.

When he proposed, a year later, it felt right. It felt like a piece that fits neatly into a puzzle. Without fireworks or fanfare. We married the same way. Without question marks. On Feb. 14th.

13

Closure: The consuming need to meet one last time

∞

In almost every story in this book, and with each main character, there is one common element. The need for closure. The yearning to see the ex, one last time, to see their once-familiar and precious face, to hear their gorgeous voice say to us one last time that you mattered. You: individually. You: as a couple. To hear that what you had was important to them too.

But in all the stories you have read in this book and all the experiences you or your friends may have had, how often have you found someone *actually getting closure* from their ex?

This burning need to see them one last time – let me give you a preview.

If, after all that happened, all the times you cried yourself into exhaustion or went through days feeling numbed, you're stuck on wanting to see them to get closure... Hold on. Do not act on it. Remember: When in doubt, do nothing.

Take your mind back to when you were a kid. Imagine you were watching a film with your family and a disturbing scene began. Your parent or older sibling's immediate response was to tell you to cover your eyes. It's a primal instinct to want to protect someone we love. *Why would you not show yourself the same self-love?*

Self-love is not just something for memes or life coaches to give gyaan on. It has to be put into practice by you. You know what still triggers you. Why voluntarily put yourself through pain? The way Sofia did in 'Moth to a flame' and Yash did in 'Controlled chaos'. They chose to click on the live link to watch their ex get married. Knowing fully the ex *chose someone else* over them. That is self-inflicted torture. Or to keep stalking the ex on their socials, to wring out updates on them, to keep reading old texts, to listen to voice texts…it is hard-core emotional atyachar. Except – you are now doing it to yourself. It is not the ex doing it to you. You *have a choice* in it.

What you hope they'll say to give you closure isn't going to happen.

Think you had something really special? Major sparks? Attraction means *nothing* without intention. Chemistry means *nothing* without commitment. Words mean f-ing *nothing* without actions to show they are meant. Love is a decision. And the bottom-line is: their actions showed that *they chose to leave.*

When they needed to show you that the relationship mattered, they bailed. The commitment to build together, to work through whatever comes, to make you a priority, not an option, was not there. They made a choice to exit. And you're expecting truth and clarity from the escape artist?

To *fall in love* is not what lasts the course, because

it's just as easy *to fall out of love.* It may sound harsh, again, I wish I didn't have to say this, but I do. Love is a choice and *your ex chose to exit.* For whatever reasons. That's not important. We tried to understand them, their attachment styles, their traumas, their beyond-tolerable issues sometimes (like the narcissistic personalities), and we tried to understand ourselves too. We allowed for the possibility that it wasn't even that your ex was a bad person. Maybe *at that point in time* you were not right for each other. It was not meant to be. But *they chose to exit.* You have to remember, especially now, that *you have a choice. To love and protect yourself from here on.* And not to sabotage your healing in this craving for closure.

What *will* they say if you chase and beg to meet, for one last time? In the story, 'Uncomfortably numb', what did Rakhi achieve by asking Kaushik to meet her? He was the one who had once chased after her, love-bombed her, made promises of a shared love and career in the music industry, then after they had sex, he ghosted her completely. If that wasn't already like a badly written movie, he then had the audacity to meet her, tell her he's marrying someone else and even suggest that they could continue to meet and have sex; except it would have to be at her place. How can a meeting like that give closure or help with a person's already low self-esteem? You think your ex is not like that? Or that you'll wheedle answers or an apology out of them? Really? *Really??*

To understand why you won't get real answers, imagine you're the uninvested one.

Think of a time when someone was crazy about you but

you couldn't reciprocate their feelings. It happens, right? No matter how much you liked, admired, felt affection, even tenderness towards that person; maybe even wished you could reciprocate their feelings, but you couldn't. Love isn't something that can be forced.

What if that person had asked to meet you because they were heartbroken over you? They needed to get closure, and understand why you couldn't love them. Could you *really* tell them why? Sometimes the reasons may not even be solid ones but they are valid all the same. It could be that you thought while some things felt right about the person, they were just excruciatingly boring or they spoke like a female Arnab or were too full of themselves or self-obsessed with a capital S, drowning you with an average of Seventy Selfies per day or that they were ambivalent about Trump (shriek!), or killed you with anecdotes that *they* were hugely animated about but *to you* they were the equivalent of melatonin in high doses, so much so that you struggled to stay awake to laugh politely now and then, or maybe they were a little too fragrant but not in a good way, more like dal left out overnight on a summer night in Delhi, or they were cheapskates and loved to book a meal at a swish restaurant, then always held back to let you pay, or that those same lips that looked quite sexy on the DP on the dating app felt much too blubbery when they were planted upon yours...or...or...or...maybe it would all have been fine and proceeded down the path of true love...if on your first long drive, when they slowed down the car, you thought it was for a big kiss but instead he proudly offered to give you a sneak peek of his 'big boy'.

Did you even want to get into the reasons why it ain't working for you when that person angrily/sulkily/broken-heartedly demanded to meet one more time to ask you 'Whyyy?'

Why can't you love them back? Jokes apart, would you tell them what you actually feel, especially if the disenchantment happened after you had been involved for some time? Or is it more likely you would choose to be kind and not really spell out what changed it for you?

Stop expecting to rekindle love with a person who checked out long ago.

Most people do not want to take responsibility or accept that they are guilty of being heartless or cruel or selfish or weak, delusional and confused children, parading as adults. Especially when the issues are hard core, like cheating or suddenly discovering they are commitment-phobic or blaming their coming-out-of-nowhere changed behaviour on 'trust issues' in hindsight. People would rather avoid any confrontation where they may feel cornered. How will it help you to insist on a meeting where you put in effort to look and smell good or show them how sad you feel or go heavy on the drama? You know it actually counts for nothing. Do you want pity sex? (If you had great sex earlier, congratulations, at least you experienced it. Park that memory as one to return to much later.) But really, pity sex will only make you wake up feeling lousier. So whyyy?

Surely, you're not looking to cop out on yourself and what you deserve in love, by settling for pity love? I call it cushion-cover love. Fake words that are being said to cushion the blow for you and act as a cover for them to look better in their own eyes. Come onnn. You're smarter than that. Wake up and smell the bullshit.

I really wish there was a way I could make things better for you. But the only thing a closure call or meeting will do is reopen and feed that craving-validation-addiction and take you right back into settling for crumbs and self-loathing. Please, love yourself a little, protect yourself and refuse to re-open wounds that are healing.

If they wanted to, they would not have chosen to leave. They would not have chosen to do the things they did. But they did it, even when they knew it would leave you feeling shattered. They made that choice. Now you make yours.

Before you give your ex another chance, whisper to yourself: 'Reheated McDonald's fries'.

Fries are lovely when they're crisp and golden and fresh, right out of the fryer. But allow them to cool down and get limp and give them a go again? Eh oh! You still want to put that unappetising, unhealthy crap into your system (puns intended)? For what joy? *Time-vasool?* Just because you invested time in that relationship, you want to go down a road leading to a dead-end? Especially if nothing has changed. Look, if you are or were in a marriage, and if there are children involved, I'd hope that you have already given counselling and couple/personal therapy a whole-hearted try. But if after everything, you see no change, especially *if the insignificant-other is a narc, don't expect them to give you closure,* let alone an about-turn.

In Italian, there's a phrase called Cavoli Riscaldati.

'Cavoli' meaning cabbage and 'riscaldati' meaning reheated. In other words, reheated cabbage. It means attempting to revive an unworkable, already failed relationship with an ex. Sorry to put you off cabbage and McDonald's leftovers and blind hopes to revive *thakka hua* (energy-less) *ex-pired* relationships for life – but if I've succeeded, you're welcome!

Face the feelings. Feel them fully. Be like a buffalo.

We know what happened cannot be reversed, yet we stay in denial, in hope. That you won't have to face what you know is coming. That you can continue pretending it was all a misunderstanding and this scary, lonely feeling will go away on its own. That's not possible.

A break-up is like a major storm in our lives. Contrary to what we may think, when the storm hits us, our only option isn't just to move away from it. By denying and fighting back our feelings, we think we're numbing ourselves. But the storm is already here. By avoiding facing it, hoping to outrun it, we continue to be in the orbit of the storm for a much longer time.

Be like a buffalo. What's that supposed to mean? David Kessler, an expert on grief, studied buffaloes for a long time. He says that when there's a storm coming, buffaloes head into it. They know that this way they will face the storm for a shorter time. You need to be like a buffalo, turn to the storm; feel the full impact of the feelings inside you that have been waiting to be acknowledged. You need to honour the feelings. Let the emotions wash over you, storm you. *You have already survived the worst part; the breakup. You will survive this.*

Processing is a process that can't be rushed.

We sometimes hold back our feelings, thinking if the dam bursts, we won't be able to stop crying. We fear a rage we have been bottling up. Let that rage burst through. There's a song by Gary Allan called 'Every storm (runs out of rain)'. Please believe that it will. In the history of storms, anywhere in the world, has it ever happened that a storm doesn't end? Exactly. More importantly, you need to release your bottled-up emotions, because otherwise they are sitting inside, doing more damage than you can imagine. Anxiety and stress from suppressing your emotions, especially anger, can lead to serious health issues like cancer, heart problems and autoimmune issues. Kessler says, 'Anger is a bodyguard for pain.' What led to that anger? What emotion is sitting suppressed below it? It could be sadness, at something that came and went away; or something we never had, much before that break-up; or that childhood need that was denied to us. By being like the buffalo, and facing the storm, we come to terms with the loss.

How do you face the storm? By allowing for space and silence – from overstimulation, from devices, and from too many opinions, even of well-meaning people. Therapy, being in nature and being with yourself is a good way to let your inner voice be heard. For me, walks work wonders. I have to discipline myself to keep the phone on flight mode. No distractions, just the physical therapy of falling into a rhythm, observing things, the changes in the trees, the squirrels going about their play, the shifting sunlight, street vendors wrapping up. When you start noticing without actually paying attention to anything specific, the emotions push through the fog. Try and find your own turning-inwards process, whether it's in pranayama (breath work) or meditation, etc.

So what if you are sitting in a park or in your car or bus and the tears flow? So what? It is not about self-pity or feeling sorry for yourself or feeling embarrassed at feeling those feelings. These are necessary tears. Good tears. They're tears of love for yourself.

Just feel for yourself. Feel the feeling fully. No feeling is final.

Heartbreak is a certainty of life. Logic, philosophy, music all help the process of healing. But what it comes down to is this. *It is not your mind that is broken. It is your heart. You need to go into your heart to heal the painful emotions.* How can anything new enter your life unless you've removed those sharp shards of emotions that keep poking at your heart? The process of feeling your feelings is bound to be painful. That's why it is compared with a storm.

Rainer Maria Rilke, poet, writes: 'Let everything happen to you. Beauty and terror. Just keep going. No feeling is final.' Through all the dull, restless, angry, sad days, remember that. Mathew Hussey, relationship expert, says we must look at feeling sorry for ourselves as *feeling for ourselves.* Isn't that beautiful? Cut the word 'sorry' out of it, and finally you allow yourself to feel for yourself. The idea of being in the storm is not to judge yourself or kick yourself for being a fool.

Fine, you were that person once who never stopped making allowances for them. And okay, fine, you didn't see that you had become a doormat or voiceless then. Love does different irrational things to us. We become someone we can barely recognise. The important thing is yes, you did all that, but *you are not that person now.* Whether you can see it yet or not, you are already different from who you were. Murakami says, 'And once the storm is over, you won't remember how you made it through, how you managed to survive. You won't even be sure, whether the storm is really over. But one thing is certain. When you come out of the storm, you won't be the same person who walked in. That's what this storm's all about.' Think of yourself as that resilient buffalo, standing bravely while the storm rages around you. You feel every strong wind, every stinging slap of rain mixed with your tears, and you will get through it. Yes, you are changed as a person for the experience. But the change also brings good with it.

The closure was in how they made you feel at the end.

That chapter in your life has ended. Re-reading previous pages won't take you forward in your story. Turn the page. Whether it's locking up a shop at the end of the day or curtain call after a performance, closure signifies the ending. But real life doesn't come with a defined ending. It is lived in a continuum. Any words, explanation or, if you're lucky, an apology of some kind for their behaviour is still only a rehashing of the past and can't undo the past. Their actions told you what the truth was. They didn't care enough to work through the issues. Their feelings towards you were fickle. They didn't have the courage to treat you with the love you deserved.

The distancing from you was the closure. The energy-less replies when they had already checked out but stayed on only superficially, was the closure. The humiliation of deceiving you, cheating on you and you being the last to find out was the closure. The agreeing to marry someone else the parents pushed them to was the closure. All the professed love that preceded it is irrelevant. Those final actions spoke. And they told you: The End.

Move on. It doesn't mean you have forgotten that experience. It means you had a lesson to learn from it. And the lesson is always to love yourself (preferably with newly gifted ex-ray vision from the universe).

Own responsibility for past choices. To choose your future regrets better.

Søren Kierkegaard, the philosopher, says that whether you marry or don't marry, you'll likely regret both. Or as we say in Hindi: *Shaadi ka laddoo…jo khaye woh pachhtaye… jo na khaye woh bhi pachhtaye.* Funny, but so true.

Then there's Christopher Hitchens, a journalist, who says, *'You have to choose your future regrets.'* I love this statement because please notice, h*e uses the word choose.* We choose, we make a judgement call, *we have personal agency – even when we face unavoidable consequences.*

It's a powerful way of looking at whatever cards we're dealt or mistakes we make. It empowers us to know that while regret is part of being human, the future regrets we will have can come from our sense of agency. It's like saying, ok, I made that choice and well, that's the way it turned out. At least we accept our role in it, versus staying stuck in a victim mindset.

In college, in Economics, I studied something called 'opportunity cost'. Basically, *anything we choose comes at the cost of another opportunity we didn't choose.* What's that got to do with heartbreak? Regardless of how brilliant a decision looks at a point in time, there will always be paths not taken with their potential 'what if' scenarios. If you hadn't said yes to that first date with your ex, you might still have been regretting it, stuck in another boring relationship, thinking of 'what if'. You chose to go on that date, one thing led to another, and here you are, with other regrets!

While we can't avoid regret entirely, *we can choose which regrets we're willing to live with.* So, remind yourself again and again, that you are the Main Character in your life story. It is not about the secondary character, the ex who came and went.

Own your decisions and their consequences, rather than looking at life as a passive participant and feeling stuck in what happened. If you accept that somewhere in all this, you too made some mistakes; maybe you ignored some red flags and still chose to love him/ her. Even when those decisions led to difficult outcomes, by owning your decisions, you have reclaimed Main Character energy. At least now, you know what matters to you. What you are willing to sacrifice. What risks you are willing to take. At least going forward, in the next chapter of your story, you can live more intentionally.

From here on, be more mindful about your decisions, they will shape your future regrets.

This is a good time to add, if you're thinking of jumping into another relationship, or getting into quick-succession revenge sex after the break-up – nooooooo. NO. That's like trying to ride a bike with trainer wheels off, while you're still learning to find your balance. For sure, it'll lead to a crash and future regrets that'll do your healing no good. It'll be your past experience times x. Ex to the power of ex'es.

The impermanence of everything and things to carry forward.

I know, it's not as if everything can be seen in black and white. The relationship you had was real, it brought you so much; perhaps the discovery of your bodies, of touch (and how unforgettable that memory can be), emotional intimacy, joy and confusion and an untimely end sometimes (as with Tarika with her first love, Jude, and then with Nayan in 'Flights of fancy'). You are left feeling raw, bereft, like the loneliest person on earth whose one true soul connection was snatched away. The hardest thing in life is letting go of someone you love. But it doesn't change the part about choosing your future regrets. Even when you have had to release a loved one for whatever reasons or circumstances out of your control, you still have a choice. To stay stuck in the past constantly harking back to what you lost, *or* to let go with gratitude and hold space for the good memories.

Our expectations of a permanent love inevitably fall short. That's how life is, sadly. The ability to choose our future regrets gives us power. Instead of fighting the fact that everything is transitory and in change, choose to accept. The credits don't roll in real life, to say here is where it ends, at the start of the happily ever after. But don't forget...

The story is about you; you are the main character.

Don't make your life story a *rondu* weepy sad story. Give it some kickass, inspiring, main-character energy!

Others are going to come, stay for a bit, leave their impact, leave memories and lessons, but *the story with you as the main character continues.* Love, probably more than one big love over time, will enter and sooner or later exit. In the story 'Just vibing', Gazid Ali tells Shubra, 'There are many beautiful people out there.' There is truth to that. Picture *abhi baaki hai, dost.*

When the time is right, you'll find your emotional walls coming down. You *will discover other beautiful relationships.* Yes, they too will ebb and flow, bring you other precious moments, transient but no less real. There's beauty in witnessing yourself coming out of the numb, heartbroken haze and starting to feel a bittersweet gratitude for the fleeting wonder of it all.

Can someone else come and give you this understanding, this real closure that you need? Of acceptance to keep the good memories, without being clouded by nostalgia into forgetting the crappy parts? Of course not.

Only you can close that door.

Only *you* can, for a change, turn those loving, forgiving thoughts you have about that ex, to yourself.

Only *you* can accept in your heart that neither of you was perfect. They were not. Just as you are not.

Only *you* can tell yourself: Our lives overlapped but I

understand that now our journeys go our separate ways.'

Only you can see that your resentments are like a hot coal burning your hands as long as you hold onto them.

Only you can now choose to release them.

Matter can neither be created nor destroyed. Neither can energy. Or love.

When I lost my father, whom I love beyond any words can convey, I really struggled to make sense of things, to find answers, but nothing could close that ache of *not knowing for sure what happens* after death, if we would ever meet again. All the wise words I read felt like generalisations. I kept hoping for some kind of epiphany.

One morning I sat up in bed remembering something we studied in school. '*Matter can neither be created nor destroyed.*' It felt like an aha! moment to me. I share it with love and compassion and no delusions of trying to be a guru in any way. I hope it helps you make sense of your loss.

Some 236 years ago, after a series of rigorous experiments, Lavoisier concluded that 'matter can neither be created nor destroyed'. Later Einstein built on it. They prove that while matter itself can be converted into energy, the *total mass-energy* of a closed system remains conserved. For example: *Melting ice:* If you weigh a sealed container with ice, allow the ice to melt into liquid water, then weigh it again, the mass remains constant. The state of matter changes, but no mass is lost or gained. Another example: *Dissolving sugar in water:* When sugar dissolves in water, the sugar molecules disperse in the water, but the total mass of the sugar and water solution remains the same as the sum of the individual masses before mixing.

What's that got to do with heartbreak? My take on it: I believe that the love you gave, the moments you had, the energy of the love you shared doesn't disappear just because it changed form, or that now you both walk on separate paths.

The energy that was created from your relationship hasn't vanished. It exists. It will come back to you, in some other form. Let it go with love.

How? A suggestion, borrowing from my life again. My father, a believer in astrology, had asked me to stay vegetarian on one day of the week. When he died unexpectedly, after a while the compulsory vegetarian day started to feel difficult. I wanted to be free of it but I couldn't ask him, could I? Nor could I just end it. I asked a family friend for a way out. He suggested making a private ceremony of it; to tell myself that with that ceremony I lovingly end this commitment.

You could give yourself a small private ceremony too, to finally close the door on this relationship. It could be a solitary walk or coffee at a place that meant something to you both. You could do something symbolic if you wish, like give away the mementos you held on to, to a charity. Or write a farewell letter, add old letters, cards, photos. Somewhere on the walk, burn it all safely.

Then, with a few quiet words of gratitude for the good memories which no one can take away from you, take a deep breath.

Take another. And then another. Release that relationship to the universe. The love will return. In a

way and time you least expect it to.
Walk free. Walk lighter. Walk head held high.
You owe nothing to anyone except yourself. And that is to live well.

The *Heartbreak Unfiltered* Album

'Music is there for us to feel less alone.' Adele

Scan the codes below to listen to the exclusive *Heartbreak Unfiltered* album that I've put together for you. There are two playlists within this album.

Side A

Heartbreak: Let it all out

I recommend that you set yourself a time limit of 15 minutes max to listen to the songs from this playlist.

Listen on shuffle or skip to whichever songs you love, let yourself feel the emotions the music is bringing up. If you feel like crying, don't hold back. Music has the power to give us catharsis as well as comfort. Make this your me-time to work through the heartbreak with music. Then put a hard stop to it when the 15 minutes are up.

Tell yourself, today's sadness quota is up. Be strict with yourself!

Side B

I'm bigger than my heartbreak

Sometime in the day, schedule 15 minutes of listening to music from the second playlist. 15 minutes is the minimum time I recommend you must listen to this empowering selection of music. There's no maximum limit to letting this music lift you up. If possible, go out for a brisk walk or a run if your health permits it, or go cycling or on a drive while listening to these songs. Not only will you return feeling lighter inside, you may even come back inspired to smile a little more than you have been lately.

With a big hug from me,
Milan

Thanks Unfiltered

A year ago, just like that, I lost vision in one eye. Over several surgeries, I regained it somewhat. More important, I also gained a lot to be grateful for. The vision loss turned out to be an eye-opener. I was able to see my life with clarity and find purpose in pushing through the tough time. Completing this book, which has been ten years in the researching and writing, became the one thing that kept me going. It is proof that we can refuse to be a victim when life lets us down. We can use the experience as our act of resistance and create something from the good that is also coming our way. I have a lot of people to thank.

Dr Radhika Tandon: For the unflappable strength, solidarity, and expert judgement in giving me back my vision. And faith in humanity.

Dr Rohan Chawla: For the quiet brilliance, infinite patience and occasional smile that helped me dare to hope.

Dibakar Ghosh: For believing in the book and in half-blind me. For the sparkling edit calls from your car, your razor-sharp mind, lightning-swift decisions, and ability to keep the macro, micro and human aspects – all in perfect balance.

Jerry Pinto, Shubha Mudgal, Mallika Dua, Santosh Desai and Sharif D. Rangnekar: For your brilliance, integrity, and the work you do. For making the time to read '*Heartbreak Unfiltered*' and your generous words for this book. I'm deeply grateful.

Preeti Gill: For nudging me to Rupa Publications and DG, my commissioning editor. What a happy match you made for this book.
Shatarupa Dhar: For the sharp eye, spirit of partnership and agile mind that thinks on many tracks to beautifully converge with mine. The comments in tracks – pure joy!
Padma Pegu: For the keen listening, understanding and mature copyediting of this book with its multiple narrative voices.
Madhusmita Kondepudi, Anshita Asnani and Dr. Shalini Mullick: For the patient listening, fearless feedback and the much needed 5 a.m. shots in the arm. From opinions on book titles, cover designs, random excerpts – between you girls and our overlapping sleep cycles across time zones, I've got all bases covered.
Bhupesh Luther, Abhijeet Chakraborty, Poonam Augustine, and Geetanjali Kapoor: For your strong cover designs, warmth and support under impossibly tight deadlines.
Thank you, Anshita, especially: For your indefatigable spirit, stunning design aesthetics, the poignant matchsticks cover concept, and the belonging with which you've held this book.
Special thanks Poonam: For the author picture from our beautiful, lazy lunch in Goa. I'll be using it for a long time.
Thank you, Abhijeet: For your help on all matters of art. And from the heart, as you always do.
Nidhi Mahesh, Manish Sinha, Rahul Bidappa, Superna Nagpal Chopra: For pitching in, weighing in – and on crunch timelines. It means a lot.

Vidur Vohra: For the incisive comments and willing ear to listen to my stories.
Krishna Vohra: For the pithy feedback on everything, much in Nana's style to 'Keep it short and keep it mild.'
Aradhana Lal, Ratna Mathur, Ritoo Jhha, Rajan Bhavnani, Renu Prasad, Sonia Kumar, Nicky Jagtiani: For opening your homes and hearts to me.
Shama Bhakhri: For showing me home is not a place, but the space you make in your heart for someone. You always said, 'Come and write your next book in my house, Milan.' I am so glad I did, and we got that precious time together. I wish you were here to see it.
Gautam Dalwani: For the unfailing support on hospital trips and all that I turn to you for.
My family, by blood and by choice: For helping me weather the storm that this year was – in ways I can't begin to list here. Your names may not be in this book but I will not forget.

Most cherished: For each of you who trusted me with your stories; without them this book would not be what it is.
Sharing your truth takes courage
and also gives it to people in ways we will never know.
Your resilience is someone else's hope.

Resources

Ainsworth, Mary S., and John Bowlby, 'An Ethological Approach to Personality Development', *American Psychologist*, Vol. 46, No. 4, 1991, 333 – 341, https://doi.org/10.1037/0003-066X.46.4.333.

Brummelman, Eddie, Sander Thomaes, Stefanie A. Nelemans, Bram Orobio de Castro, Geertjan Overbeek, and Brad J. Bushman, 'Origins of Narcissism in Children', Vol. 112, No. 12, 2015, 3659 – 3662, https://doi.org/10.1073/pnas.1420870112.

Chapman, Gary, *The 5 Love Languages: The Secret to Love That Lasts*, Moody Publishers, Chicago, IL, 2008.

The 5 Apology Languages: The Secret to Healthy Relationships, Northfield Publishing Group, Woodmere, NY, 2022.

Chödrön, Pema, *Taking the Leap: Freeing Ourselves from Old Habits and Fears*, Shambhala, Boulder, CO, 2010.

Fisher, Helen E., Lucy L. Brown, Arthur Aron, Greg Strong, and Debra Mashek, 'Reward, Addiction, and Emotion Regulation Systems Associated With Rejection in Love', *Journal of Neurophysiology*, Vol. 104, No. 1, 2010, 51 – 60, https://doi.org/10.1152/jn.00784.2009.

'How to Quickly Get Over a Breakup - TWR Podcast #67', YouTube, https://www.youtube.com/watch?v=yYa7ppvMbos.

Kessler, David, and Katherine Twells, 'Shining Light into the Dark with David Kessler', *Coca-Cola CMO Leadership Summit*, 21 November 2022, https://tinyurl.com/59y48h53.

Kessler, David, and Matthew Hussey, 'Matt Monday: Healing from Heartbreak and Grief w/David Kessler', *Matthew Hussey*, https://tinyurl.com/bdfu4t2n.

Kübler-Ross, Elisabeth, and David Kessler, *On Grief and Grieving*, Scribner, New York, NY, 2014.

Langeslag, Sandra J.E., and Michelle E. Sanchez, 'Down-regulation of love feelings after a romantic break-up: Self-report and electrophysiological data', https://pubmed.ncbi.nlm.nih.gov/28857575/.

Murakami, Haruki, *Kafka on the Shore*, Vintage, New York, NY, 2005.

Murakami, Haruki, *What I Talk About When I Talk About Running*, Vintage, New York, NY, 2019.

'Narcissistic Personality Disorder', *Mayo Clinic*, 6 April 2023, https://tinyurl.com/4us7mm6k.

'Narcissistic Personality Disorder', *Merck Manual*, August 2024, https://tinyurl.com/mvsram9m.

Virk, Naheed, 'Tu Dard Bhi Dua Bhi Tu Zakhm Bhi Dawa Bhi', *Rekhta*, https://tinyurl.com/2wwe76e5.